The Handbook of

WOMEN'S MYSTERIES

Practices to Reclaim

Our Ancient

Gifts and Powers

DR. CHRISTINE R PAGE

The Handbook of Women's Mysteries
Practices to Reclaim our Ancient Gifts and Powers
Copyright © 2017 by Christine R. Page, M.D. All rights reserved.

Meditations are not suitable for use when driving or managing heavy machinery
First published April 2017 in the United States of America

ISBN 10: 0-9978143-2-2
ISBN 13: 0-978-0-9978143-2-3

Word Count: 32,520

www.christinepage.com **e-mail**: info@christinepage.com
Facebook: Dr.ChristinePage

Credits
Editor: Anne Dillon
Artist: Eran Cantrell
Music: Steve Roach
Cover plus chapter title pages: Cover of 'Our Old Home' author Nathaniel Hawthorne, binding designer Sarah Whitman, 1891, Boston Public Library; dc:iden=0604000244. Wording added by Dr. Christine Page.
Bowl image: Iranian bronze bowl located LACMA public domain
http://collections.lacma.org/search/site/M.76.97.399

This book is dedicated to all girls and women—past, present and future— and the men who love them.

In honor of the Great Mother—in all her forms—and the love and wisdom always present to us if we open our hearts, empty our wombs and root ourselves into Mother Earth

There's nothing more beautiful in the Universe, than a woman in her power

—Leland Landry (author's husband)

TABLE OF CONTENTS

Stand Strong, Be Heard, Feel Free

Are you eager to embody all that is luscious, natural and gorgeous about being female but don't know where to start? Do want to enjoy your body rather than constantly thinking about ways to change it? Welcome to this handbook of women's mysteries, written for women and girls of all ages. Full of invaluable advice for healing, empowerment, and creativity, it taps into practices and teachings that were, in ancient times, taught to all girls from puberty onward. The teachings went underground 3,500 years ago with the rise of the patriarchy but are now revealing themselves again, as waves of girls and women step forward to be seen, known, and respected as the leaders of the future.

Today, you are recognized and celebrated as one of these courageous and powerful women!

In the past, we would only have been taught the wisdom and practices appropriate to our age. But now, with humanity on the precipice of change, many keepers of ancient mysteries believe they should be shared with a wider audience if we are going to birth a brand new world where cooperation, peace, and prosperity are available to all humanity and where we once again respect and harmonize with Mother Earth.

Who are better equipped to birth a new world?

Women! This is why there is a tsunami of interest in women's empowerment, not by becoming mini-men but by embodying the sacred mysteries of the feminine.

Each chapter of this handbook builds upon the next, reflecting the natural passage from blossoming womanhood, through creativity and mothering, finally arriving at the golden years of wisdom and transformation. To enhance the embodiment of the teachings some of the chapters include questions to stir your thoughts and feelings; for feeling leads to healing. Feel free to use this handbook as a journal where you can go back and add insights from self-reflection, dreams, memories, notes and affirmations. You can write or draw your insights which can be then shared within the sacred space of a women's group. The more we communicate as women, the more healing we bring to the world.

I see each chapter as an intimate journey into womanhood. Take time to absorb what you read and experience, recognizing that each exercise is designed to open the way for clarity, healing, and transformation, which may need days or even weeks to fully embody. Initially, you may decide to focus on the particular area of the book relevant to your needs. But I suggest that at some point you read *all* the chapters, as there are nuggets of gold on every page that you may wish to share with your friends, mother, sisters, children, and grandchildren.

This handbook complements my earlier inspirational book the *Healing Power of the Sacred Woman,* which covers each subject in greater depth, giving historic, esoteric, and everyday meaning to a woman's health, creativity, and fertility.

Mysteries

Every religion and culture has its mysteries; beliefs that are difficult to explain or define through our human mind, given that they exist in the world of spiritual truths and archetypes. These mysteries are usually passed down through the telling of stories or myths when the logical mind is switched off, allowing the intuitive heart to listen. Creation myths are the most common, attempting to explain something that, even today our scientists are *still* trying to understand. Many cultures believe that the source of all creation is feminine not masculine, often calling her the Great Mother, a term you'll hear throughout the handbook.

The best known female mysteries in the western world are the Eleusinian Mysteries, which continued as an annual event in Eleusis, Greece, for over 1,500 years. They followed the story of the descent into the underworld of an innocent young girl named Kore (also known as Persephone), the ensuing grief of her mother Demeter, and Persephone's eventual resurrection as a fully mature woman. Great secrecy surrounded these mysteries, although it is known that the female participants went through several physical and emotional purification processes before descending into the underworld to reconnect to their inherent power, wisdom, and creative inspiration: the mystical essence of a woman's menstrual cycle.

The honoring of this ritual benefited not only the participant but also strengthened the collective awareness and creative abundance of all women. For women are bound together by three amazing truths: we embody the power of love, we flow with intrinsic rhythm, and we are the true spiritual leaders of this world.

Stepping into Mystery

Being female means there's no need to develop our biceps or intellect to be powerful. Our bodies are already primed at birth with abundant creativity and magical powers, while our minds have access to deep wells of wisdom. These gifts are activated at puberty, but sadly, without knowledge of the mysteries, most women access only a very small percentage of the power and creative opportunities that are readily available to us when we work in rhythmic cooperation with our body and the creative genius of Mother Earth.

Since the mysteries were lost to us with the rise of the patriarchy, around 1500 BCE, there are few role models alive today who embody the persona of a fully empowered woman. To begin the change, I would love to see every girl and woman respecting themselves and their bodies, refusing to allow anybody to disrespect them, whether by words, looks, or physical actions. Respect is a fundamental right of all people and always begins with us.

Some Juicy Thoughts

1. We women are only using a *small percentage of the power* available to us by birthright.

2. As females, we have *innate gifts* which, when fully embraced, would change the face of humanity's evolution, bringing peace, cooperation, and well-being to all.

3. *Women are the soil for all new birth*; by letting go of outdated beliefs, healing old wounds, and having compassion for ourselves, we heal not only our ancestors but the children still to follow.

4. For centuries we've been disconnected from Mother Earth's fiery dragon energy, which is our innate creative power. *It is time to reawaken our inner dragon.*

5. It's predicted that: *A thousand years of peace will come when women heal their hearts.*

This Sacred Space is your friend, waiting to hear how you feel after reading about the amazing female gifts that live within you, awaiting full expression! Write your thoughts below:

CHAPTER 1

My Story of the Feminine

Qualifying as a medical doctor in London in 1978, I specialized in pediatrics, gynecology, and obstetrics before settling into general practice. Having delivered and cared for hundreds of babies, I can still see the joy on the faces of the parents when presented with a beautiful healthy child, as well as the concern and united effort of the doctors and nurses when the health of the mother or newborn was at risk. I remember numerous occasions when I was present to a woman's courage as she faced the emotional trauma of being told she had cancer, and my feelings of helplessness and indignation when listening to stories of the sexual and physical abuse of women and children.

Travelling the world as healthcare provider and teacher for many years, I've been privy to the inner dreams, hopes, wounds, and fears of thousands of amazing women. I've heard stories of insults against womanhood that have turned my stomach and tales of courage and resilience that have made me weep with joy. I've been part of a group of women who have changed consciousness just by their collective strength of "*compassionate togetherness.*" And I have marveled as women willingly lay aside their personal desires—the "me"—for the sake of the "we," to ensure a healthy and peaceful world for future generations.

Raised amongst strong, insightful, and compassionate women, I saw the men in their lives shower them with love and respect, honored to be able to support such inner creative beauty. My husband agrees, saying: *There's nothing more beautiful in the universe than a woman in her power.* I meet many men who want to support their wives, daughters, and girlfriends in reconnecting to their feminine but are unclear how to help and often are told: "*You should know!*" Without any disrespect, men are fairly simple; they just want to hear what we want and then they will go into action.

But our general uncertainty about our identity as women is causing them great confusion. My aim is not to change men but to help every woman and girl to see herself as a queen bee, or gorgeous goddess just waiting to be adored.

I attended an all girls' high school and then a medical college that had initially been created to be just for women, in the days when women were not allowed to attend medical schools with men. These all-female settings allowed me to see how women behave when they are truly in their power. They are gracious, compassionate, and open-minded, without the need to compete through words or actions as mini-men, for they embody all the qualities of feminine power and know they will always be respected.

Throughout my years in the healthcare profession, it has become clear to me that there's a strong link between our thoughts and the appearance of physical illness, and that many illnesses are a wake-up call from the soul, telling us it's time to change. Throughout this handbook, you'll see my thoughts on the underlying message of disease. As well, I offer suggestions to enhance one's self-care program. These suggestions aim to both prevent disease as well as to ease symptoms that may already be present. All of this is to be used alongside (not instead of) orthodox or complementary therapies.

* * *

Today, as many women find success along their chosen path, we're witnessing increasing levels of equality between the genders. Sadly, many only reach such parity by disconnecting from the very things that define us as women, in particular our female rhythm. I'm often asked: *Why write a book just for women? Surely we all possess masculine and feminine traits?*

My answer: *Only women are lucky enough to have breasts, a womb, ovaries, and a vagina—and that's why I'm delighted to be a woman!*

It's time to roar: *I am woman, know me!*

As our greatest friend, our body expresses the disconnection from our feminine rhythm through dis-ease, both physical and emotional. As a result, amongst the female population:

- 60 percent complain of premenstrual symptoms (PMS).

- 80 percent experience menopausal problems.

- Heart disease is the number 1 killer in the United States.

- One in fifteen has symptoms of polycystic ovary syndrome.

- Many have uterine fibroids.

- Cancer of the breast, uterus, cervix, and ovary are far too common.

- Many engage in secretive eating, drinking and cutting disorders.

The prevalence of these illnesses reflects the fact that the collective female mind and body are seriously distressed. Things will not improve until we, as women, heed the call of our feminine spirit and choose to nurture and treasure it, as our number 1 priority. When you embrace all that you are as a beautiful and powerful woman everything will change in your life.

Let's see how much you embody female energy. Grade the present level of each feminine quality within your life today, from 1-5, where 1 strongly suggests you're spending too much time enhancing masculine

strengths, and 5 tells the whole world, you're one beautiful, sensual and powerful woman. *(Omit those qualities which are not relevant to you).* **You may wish to use a pencil so you can make changes later!**

___ *I enjoy the unique shape and curves of my body.*

___ *I demand and receive respect from men and other women.*

___ *My voice and opinions are heard.*

___ *There's equal give-and-take in all of my intimate relationships*

___ *With healthy emotional boundaries, I have energy and fun.*

___ *My sensual and sexual pleasure is fantastic.*

___ *I listen to and trust my intuition.*

___ *New seeds of exciting inspiration flow through me ready to be birthed.*

___ *My menstrual periods are easy and fulfilling.*

___ *I have no symptoms of premenstrual syndrome (PMS)*

___ *My ovaries are bursting with creativity.*

___ *I have no or minimal menopausal symptoms such as hot flushes/flashes, etc.*

___ *My breast care includes nurturing of all parts of me with huge doses of self-love.*

___ *In my postmenopausal years I'm content and creative*

___ *I love being a woman!*

CHAPTER 2

Ancestral Messages: We Are What We Believe

With so many women around the world being inspired to make a difference, we're asking: *Who am I?* We're no longer willing to merely mold ourselves into testosterone-fueled stereotypes or be pressurized into changing our appearance to support idealized views of femininity, fed to us by the media or peer pressure.

What does it mean to you to be a woman? Probably there are things that you really like about being female, while you've learned to accept and sometimes ignore other traits that you don't think you can change. These traits might include such things as unpredictable emotions, the shape of your body, or uncomfortable periods. But what if these features are not just essential to womanhood but also precious gifts?

Beliefs and perceptions about our femininity greatly influence our relationships, maternal instincts, state of well-being, and even the shape of our body. The messages we receive early in life, from both male and female relatives, are strong factors in determining the women we will become. These messages may be verbal or nonverbal. For instance, did you see your mother behave differently when alone, at work, or with her partner and family?

Think back, did you ever hear (verbally or subconsciously) the following. Write any relevant family beliefs, mottoes or sayings you heard as a child or teenager:

- *Being too powerful or assertive as a female is not okay*

- *Being a sexual and sensual woman is shameful*

- *Periods are the curse of all women*

- *You're only female if you give birth to a child*

- *The shape of your body is not okay*

- *You're dried up and finished after menopause*

In addition to beliefs we may have picked up throughout our life from relatives and acquaintances, we also inherit the perceptions of the last seven generations of female ancestors. This means that since we create beliefs to deal with emotional overload surrounding an event, something that traumatized your great-grandmother years ago is still impacting your mind and body today. For instance, if she felt abandoned when her husband died in a war, unconsciously you may have fear of committing to a relationship, in case you too are abandoned.

The good news is that when we heal or change an unhealthy belief into something that is more empowering, we heal not only the last seven generations of women but the next seven generations to come.

Here are some more questions to stir your memories; take time to reflect and to write your answers (omitting those not relevant to you at this time):

What Messages about Being Female Did You Receive In Your Childhood?

a. *What verbal (and non-verbal) messages did you receive from your relatives about being a woman?*

b. *How did you see your female relatives behave, especially in your first five years of life?*

c. *Would you consider the women in your life powerful? If so, how did they use their power?*

d. *What three adjectives describe your mother's femininity?*

e. *Were the women in your family respected and supported by the men?*

f. *Did you ever witness abuse to women—whether physical, emotional, or sexual?*

g. *Were you abused as a child or young woman—whether physical, emotional, or sexual?*

h. *Were boys and girls treated equally in your family?*

i. *Did you ever see women misuse their feminine energy, perhaps through emotional manipulation or seduction?*

j. Do you recall any stories about female relatives that were described as the 'family secret' which gave warnings against improper behavior?

k. Name three qualities that you think a female should possess if she's fully in touch with her feminine attributes. Do you have any role models in mind?

l. What expectations do you have of yourself as a woman?

Do You Enjoy Having a Woman's Body?

a. Were you a tomboy as a child? What happened after puberty?

b. Do you find it difficult to live fully in your body? Do you live in your head?

c. *Do you ever wish your body shape was different? Have you made changes to the way you look?*

d. *Have you ever had an eating disorder?*

e. *Do you or did you enjoy having menstrual periods?*

f. *Do you like your breasts? What do you like or dislike?*

g. *Has your body ever let you down?*

Clearing the Fear of Survival

Some of the deepest ancestral memories that subconsciously cause anxiety in women are those surrounding death, whether of ourselves or our children. Whether we have children or not in this life, we inherently know that the survival of our offspring is intricately dependent on our own survival and well-being. One has only to look at a family tree to see mothers and children who have died during childbirth or in early infancy, resulting in all manner of grief.

Such grief is imprinted on our psyche, even though today the risk of death during childbirth is extremely low. The process of giving birth is a profound event and—despite the claims of modern medicine—is still a miracle.

Therefore, when consulting with a woman who is infertile or has illness of the ovaries or uterus, I believe in asking the difficult questions to expose any inherited beliefs or anxieties about the risk of dying, as these underlying fears may influence our goal of achieving a successful pregnancy or healing.

Because we commonly create future realities from our beliefs, it's important to have the courage to expose all of our perceptions so we can choose which ones still nurture and honor us and which ones need to be released.

When enough women say "yes" to those beliefs that respect the true heart of womanhood, we will change the face of femininity forever!

CHAPTER 3

What Does It Mean to Be a Powerful Female?

History tells us that from approximately 35,000 to 3,000 years ago women and men lived in egalitarian societies that honored the gifts and skills of both genders. Women who fully embraced their sacred feminine powers were honored as spiritual leaders, wisdom keepers, birthers of dreams and children, and guardians of the future's peaceful prosperity. Today our ancient Grandmothers would ask:

> *Why did you ever give your power away?*
> *Who told you that you're not beautiful?*

As spiritual leaders in the past, women were responsible for deciding political, social, spiritual, and economic policies for the tribe. In many indigenous tribes, they were called Clan Mothers or Grandmothers, and they were selected to lead, not because they had grandchildren, but because they had reached a place of wisdom and detachment from personal needs and therefore could selflessly decide what was best for their people. It was clearly understood by everybody that only women knew the pain of burying a child that she'd suckled at her breast, and consequently, only women had the wisdom to decide **what was worth fighting for**.

It was the Clan Mothers who received the inspired ideas and visions that offered optimal benefit to all members of the tribe, while the men were entrusted to bring those visions and policies into manifestation.

Outwardly men were the leaders, but it was the Grandmothers who nominated and elected them, and therefore could also remove them from their position if they failed to fulfill their responsibilities. Imagine the world today if every decision involving governance was first reviewed by Clan Mothers and if every man was openly accountable to the females in his life, knowing he faced the risk of losing prestige, property, and title if he failed to live up to his promises.

When the shaman John Perkins asked the people of the Amazonian Shuar tribe to describe the most important job of women, he was told: *Telling their men when to stop*! What would you like to tell the man or men in your life to stop doing today, to create a better world for today's children and for future generations?

Being Female

We have over 35,000 years of evidence to suggest that being attractive as a woman doesn't require us to starve ourselves until we're a size 2 or look like a pre-pubertal girl. Instead our ancestors celebrated their abundant curves, their sensual juiciness, and their fertility. This Venus or feminine figurine from 24,000 years ago clearly says: *Don't even think of messing with me*!

Venus of Gagarino, found in Ukraine, 22,000 BCE (Hermitage Museum, St. Petersburg, Russia)

The Mysteries Teach Us That the Gifts of a Fully Embodied Woman Are Many and Varied. They Include Our Embodiment of the Following Qualities.

Spend time reflecting on each gift and how this applies to your own life.

1. **Loving and Connecting**

   Women are like magnets, thriving on love, cooperation, connection, support, and togetherness, knowing that this is the way to create a more peaceful and unified world. We yearn to merge with the mystery of the Great Mother, for we know this is the source of all creativity. We're more interested in the "we" rather than the "me," knowing that the strength and survival of a tribe, family, culture, or country, is dependent on women working together with compassion and caring.

2. **Wisdom Keeper**

   The wisdom we possess doesn't come from intellectual knowledge but exists as a grid or network of dragon energy that flows beneath our feet. (We will learn more about dragon energy and how to tap into it in chapter 7.) This grid contains the energetic potential for everything we can possibly manifest on this planet; eternal wisdom. Accessed through the mystery of emptiness and detachment from external sources of satisfaction, our psyche craves to return to this source of creation, for it feels like coming home.

3. **Transformative Powers**

   Because of our ability to embody this wisdom, we can see the potential in other people—what they *could* become—and we are instinctively programmed to surround them in loving, transformative juices to help them achieve fulfillment. However, to avoid frustration, it's important to remember that just because we can see someone's potential, it's *their* choice to change, not ours.

4. **Clear-Sightedness**

   Women have clear intuitive sight to see beyond the masks and veils behind which many people hide. But as you may have experienced, such vision is not always welcome, given that secrecy is still a powerful defense for many people. This is the reason why women have been called witches, for they *see and know too much.*

5. **Clearing Emotions**

   As part of our transformative process, we're able to take on and transform the emotions of others into blood, to be shed during our next menstrual period. Unfortunately, as most of us are unaware of the clearing nature of our periods (which you'll learn about in this handbook) it's not uncommon for women to become overwhelmed by emotions. Time to release those emotions, gals!

6. **Birthing**

   Giving birth to a child is a wonderful experience. But as you'll learn, every woman is fertile every month, even beyond menopause, with the ability to give birth not only to babies but also ideas and dreams!

7. **Mastering the Power of Our Inner Sexual Serpent**

   Sexual energy is a powerful magnetic force that causes us to feel excited and connected to something greater than our individual selves. Running through the Earth as dragon energy, it has the potential to become serpent energy as it makes its way up along our spine. Thirty-five hundred years ago we became disconnected from this energy and our kundalini, the serpent goddess at the base of our spine, fell asleep. It's time to reclaim and master our sexual dragon power, reawaken kundalini, and bring about profound transformation both in ourselves and in others.

8. **Inspirational Insights**

   Whether at the end of a menstrual period or during labor, orgasm, or our postmenopausal years, women have a unique ability to tap into the collective unconscious and receive the spark of life that activates new ideas and dreams, into reality.

9. **Spiritual Leaders**

   When we embrace all of these qualities, we're ready to step forward as leaders of a new world!

CHAPTER 4

What Defines Us As Women?

We All Have Babies!

Not true. Approximately 20 percent of females worldwide will reach menopause childless; approximately 50 percent by choice and 50 percent because they were unable to have a child. I'm a childless woman by choice and still recall receiving a few comments such as: *Oh, I'm sorry you don't have children; you'll never know what it is to be a real woman!* These unfortunate remarks can be extremely painful for those women who are unable to give birth. Infertility is a complex subject involving many physical and deep psychological factors. Fortunately, today attitudes are changing. Women have a greater variety of avenues to follow in the pursuit of happiness and fulfillment, which may or may not include having a family.

The belief that a woman's role in life is to procreate was very practical in the past, for it ensured the continuity and strength of the family, tribe, religion, and/or culture. However, this may be less relevant today for, you may have noticed, we're a little overpopulated on this planet at the moment!

If We Don't All Have Children Then What Do All Women Do?

Almost without exception, we all have periods and a menstrual cycle that we experience every month for approximately forty years!

This is a very long time and yet I don't remember having anniversary dinners based on the fact I'd had ten or twenty years of monthly periods, do you? Forty years of marriage is celebrated so why don't we celebrate this partnership with our periods? Most women can tell me about their first period or menarche. After that initial period, however, invariably the menstrual cycle becomes a relative nonevent—unless there are problems. I sense we don't even talk about our periods with other women, do we? Let me ask you: *What do you know about your friends' periods? Are they heavy, painful, or irregular?*

It's also my experience that if we do encounter menstrual problems, it's often other females who are more unsympathetic than men. *Stop whining! Just take the pill or have a hysterectomy,* they say.

When did women become so mean to each other?

Maybe one of the reasons we don't take more notice of our periods is because most of us are taught that the only reason to have a menstrual cycle is to become pregnant with a child. I know this belief is prevalent in many cultures, for I'm often told: *When I had my first period, there wasn't any special celebration but instead I remember being warned; "Be careful now; don't get pregnant!"*

Periods, Sex, and Pregnancy are Typically Intertwined in the Minds of Many Girls and Women, with Generous Sprinkles of Fear, Guilt, and Shame

Sadly, it's often the case that when a woman is trying to get pregnant and her period arrives like clockwork, the period becomes the enemy that defies her desires and makes her to feel like a failure.

What If Our Menstrual Cycle Is Not Merely Connected with Procreation?

Let's run the numbers:

The average birth rate per woman globally is 2.4 births

The average number of menstrual cycles per woman (from puberty to menopause) is 420 cycles

It's been suggested to me that these extra cycles give a woman plenty of potential to get pregnant. I reply that's a lot of wasted potential: 417 extra cycles! Mother Nature abhors waste.

I'd imagine if she expected us just to have two to three babies, then we'd have a couple of years of periods and then be done with them.

These figures suggest that it's time to take a new look at our menstrual cycle. What if a woman has the chance to **give birth every month**, not only to babies, but also to new creative ideas and dreams? What if women are the birthers of new consciousness, whether that appears as a baby's unique gifts or as new projects and inspirational ideas?

If I'm Postmenopausal or Have Had a Hysterectomy, Does That Mean I'm Dried Up and Finished?

Not at all! It's also not true that the reason we stop bleeding is because, as I often hear: *We're not meant to live beyond our mid-fifties.* The reality is that we're programmed to live well beyond a century. Our periods stop after approximately thirty-five to forty years because by then we should have learned to flow through a creative cycle and no longer need an outer manifestation to guide us.

Our body and mind are aligned to the rhythm and phases of the moon. This is why indigenous people prefer to call our period, our *moon-time.* The words *menarche, menses, menstrual,* and *menopause* all derive from the Latin word *mensis,* meaning "the month." All of these words originally referred to the moon's phases as measures of time. The word *period* originates from the Greek *periodos,* which means "going around," or "a cycle." The Latin name for the goddess of the moon is *luna,* which gives us the word *lunacy,* a state of mind many men believe women enter just before a period and at menopause!

Once we reach the age of fifty-four or thereabouts, the rhythm of the cycles is firmly imprinted upon our psyche, and our hormones can calm down. It is important, however, for both postmenopausal women and women who have had a hysterectomy, to continue to align to the rhythm of the moon, as described in chapter 9.

CHAPTER 5

Flowing with Female Creativity and Rhythm

Have You Ever Noticed That You Tend to Wake Up at 3:00 a.m.?

Three is the feminine number and three o'clock in the morning is seen as women's hour when the night is at its deepest and mystery surrounds us. It's the perfect time to merge with the Great Mother's wisdom and tap into her source of unlimited potential. Maybe you've heard her call and been inspired to write or draw something during this bewitching hour? Personally, when I wake up at this time, I love to acknowledge the connection and then fall asleep again, letting my dream self explore her immense caverns of creative mystery.

Continuing the theme of three, I've visited many ancient circular structures or temples that were built in honor of the feminine or Great Mother and found them to have three rooms or three levels. Our ancestors knew that to ensure fertility, prosperity, and abundance, there needs to be a rhythmic flow between three phases of a timeless cycle.

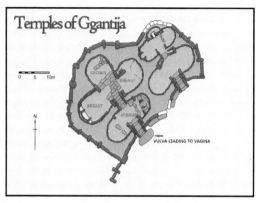

These temples of Ggantija on the tiny island of Gozo in the Mediterranean were built 5,000 years ago in the shape of a woman, to receive and transmit cosmic energies into Mother Earth. The entrance and the narrow passageway represent the vulva and vagina leading into the first large chamber, which mirrors the uterus and the ovaries. Then we move into the second large chamber, which represents the two breasts around the heart chakra, and finally we see the third chamber at the top, reflecting the head or crown chakra. Together they embrace the feminine qualities of fertility, nurturing, and inspiration.

The Creative Process Has Three Phases Aligned to the Phases of the Moon

1. **Growth and fertility (waxing moon):** active growth of new ideas, with fertile expression at the full moon

2. **Nurturing and sharing (waning moon):** celebration of achievements, sharing of wisdom, self-nurturing, and self-reflection

3. **Release and inspiration (dark moon):** clearing of the soil before receiving new inspiration around the new moon

The most powerful time for women is not the full moon, but the three dark days around the new moon, when the light of the moon is absent in the night sky. This is because female energy is mysterious, introverted, magnetic, and intuitive, thriving in environments that are hidden, dark, and without form. The three days of the dark moon include the day before the new moon, the day of the new moon, and the day after the new moon. Interestingly, once we start paying attention to our menstrual cycle, we often find that our moon-time aligns to the days of the dark moon.

Charting the Lunar Phases in Your Diary or Calendar
With so many of us living in cities where the night sky is less visible and life is so busy, it can be difficult to keep in rhythm with the moon's phases. Here's a typical moon calendar with the international symbols for the new and full moon: dark circle new moon, white circle full moon.

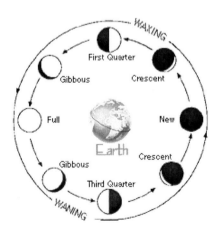

Take time now to find a diary or calendar – there are some great apps available - and highlight either your period dates or the dark moon dates so you begin to cycle with the moon again!

CHAPTER 6

The Three Faces of the Great Mother

Continuing the theme of three, the Great Mother—source of all creation—also has three faces, which are often described in mythology as the three faces of the goddess. These three aspects mirror the three phases of the creative cycle:

1. **Virgin energy** seen as creative, enthusiastic, and inspiring

2. **Mother energy** linked to nurturing, sustenance, and confidence-building

3. **Crone or dark goddess energy** associated with breakdown, death, and rebirth

Whatever our stage of life, all women journey through their inner virgin, mother, and crone once a month, whether as part of her menstrual cycle or when following the lunar cycle.

1. **Virgin energy** represents the estrogen phase of the menstrual cycle or the waxing moon

2. **Mother energy** represents the progesterone phase or the waning moon

3. **Crone energy** represents the menstrual period or dark moon.

Even though it's relatively easy to envisage an inner virgin and mother, imagining and accepting our inner crone or dark goddess is usually more difficult, especially given that she's often depicted trailing death and destruction in her wake. She is the most powerful of the three aspects of the Great Mother and is empowered with the gifts of transformation and magic. As such, she appears in many fairy tales, sometimes as the wicked witch or hag and sometimes as the wise woman or fairy godmother.

In Truth, the Crone or Dark Goddess Is the Part of Us That:

- *Has clear sight*; seeing through any masks or disguises we may wear to hide our true self.

- *Knows the truth* of who we are.

- *Embodies sexual dragon power*; possesses the *power of transformation.*

- Invites us into her cauldron so we can *die to the old way and give birth to the new.*

- *Has no fear of death*, as she sees it as the doorway to the mysterious realms of possibilities.

- *Loves us so much* that she'll create chaos in our lives to force us to change direction.

- Is very persuasive when she wants us to change our mind; *she is the sorceress.*

- Is greatly feared by the patriarchy because, being fearless of death, *she cannot be controlled.*

- Must be allowed *to be part of our life,* otherwise we'll be sorry!

In mythology, the crone or dark goddess is described as *Kali* (eating the entrails of her lover while having sex), *Lilith* (blamed for the lustful thoughts of men), *Ereshkigal* (the ugly sister of Inanna), and the Great Bear *Artemis* (who demands that you change when she says change). She is also *Mary Magdalene,* who the Christian Church attempted to banish from their teachings because she is the only one of the three faces of Mary—*Virgin Mary, Mother Mary, and Crone Mary*—that they could not control.

The name "dark goddess" reflects her comfort with living in the darkness of mystery and her ability to handle all aspects of her power, including those which are destructive, seductive, manipulative, and generally not very ladylike! If you're ready to take on your power, then you're being asked to embody the likes of Kali and Lilith, as well as the dark faces of Isis, Artemis, and Persephone.

Are there archetypal female figures - such as goddesses, female icons or even cartoon figures, which come to mind when you think of your inner virgin, your inner mother and your inner crone? Write or draw your answers below, knowing they may change as you embody the Women's Mysteries?

MY IDEA OF MY INNER VIRGIN:

MY IDEA OF MY INNER MOTHER:

MY IDEA OF MY INNER CRONE:

CHAPTER 7

Womb Power: Reawakening Your Dragon Energy

Now that we've met the three faces of our inner feminine, it's time to reacquaint ourselves with an energy that is essential to all of them but that has been almost forgotten until now: dragon energy. This female force, which naturally flows throughout the planet, is most potent when it can curl inside a round vessel such as a mountain, cave, or a well, or within our own female womb.

In fact, when our womb is full of dragon energy, it becomes our **seat of power**. Even if you've had a hysterectomy, dragon energy can still curl around the inside of your energetic womb. Trust me, when you decide to make space in your womb for this liquid fire, your persona will change forever. You'll feel more confident, your words will be heard across a crowded room, and you'll gain respect as an inspirational leader.

Dragon Power

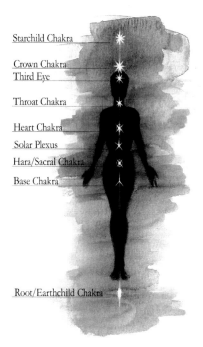

Starchild Chakra

Crown Chakra
Third Eye

Throat Chakra

Heart Chakra
Solar Plexus
Hara/Sacral Chakra

Base Chakra

Root/Earthchild Chakra

The Nine Energy Centers or Chakras (artist Eran Cantrell)

To access dragon energy we need to travel beneath our feet to a chakra that has been abandoned for far too long: *the Earthchild or root chakra.* Often confused with the base chakra at the base of our spine (where the serpent goddess, *kundalini*, sleeps), this energy center is approximately nine feet (three meters) below ground level.

It's through this root chakra that Mother Earth's pure dragon energy flows. Often portrayed in ancient creative myths as a fiery sea dragon with a serpent's tail, this golden liquid fire runs within a winding planetary grid system, along pathways known as *spirit lines, song lines, or dragon lines*, bringing eternal abundance and creativity to the planet. To harness this energy and hence increase the productivity of certain areas, our ancestors planted trees or tall standing stones in their land, piercing the earth, knowing that the dragon-serpent enjoys spiraling around any stick or pole, including our legs.

While we may not be familiar with the term *dragon-serpent energy*, its more common title is certainly well-known: *sexual energy*. But while sexual intercourse is only perceived as a pleasurable pastime or as a means of making babies, we're failing to see the sexual act in its true light. When we make love, we're tapping into a powerful creative potential that brings us healing and fulfillment far beyond the experience itself. Sexual dragon energy carries this potential and brings fertility and creative abundance to everything we see on the planet today.

This energy originally was seen as feminine—*the dragon queen*—so women in particular have a strong link to it, with the ability to draw it up through our root chakra, store it in our uterus, and use it as a source of power. Nothing grows without receiving nourishment from it, including humans. This is why many Asian cultures revere the dragon as the source of wisdom and abundance.

Dragon energy has three purposes, which align to the three faces of the Great Mother:

1. In spring and summer, it encourages growth and prosperity—*virgin energy*.

2. In fall and winter, it encourages breakdown and death—*crone energy*.

3. It carries eternal wisdom, where everything that has been and ever will be created on this Earth is already known and exists in an energetic form as the dragon energy grid. It holds the blueprint for human consciousness in its most perfect form: Heaven on Earth. When we are willing to love and be loved, the doors open to this pure potential: *mother energy*.

Our ancestors paid reverence to this dragon-serpent power, knowing there are times to build and times to let go, which reflects the cyclical nature of the sun, the moon, and the seasons. But 3,500 years ago, the incoming patriarchy was not willing to allow death and chaos to disrupt their plans and therefore they decided to banish dragon energy, denigrate all cycles (including the menstrual cycle), and punish women for being women. In some cultures, the dragon was given a masculine face, which confused the situation even further.

It was erroneously taught that dragons and serpents were evil and should be destroyed, leading to many mythological tales of heroes killing dragons supposedly *to save the innocent virgin from being eaten by the monster*; three cheers for the hero! In truth, trying to kill the dragon is as futile as attempting to prevent the onset of winter or the sun from setting, emanating from a deep masculine fear of being out of control or lost in darkness. The hero wasn't saving the virgin; he was saving himself from having to surrender to the chaotic and powerful feminine. The virginal part of us wants to be taken into the darkness to meet the dragon for only then can she transition into the crone and embrace the power of transformation and fertility, so that she may later emerge as a newly inspired female.

The hero wasn't saving the virgin; he was saving himself from having to surrender to the powerfully destructive feminine and face chaos. The virginal part of us wants to be taken into the darkness to meet the dragon for only then can she transition into the crone and embrace her innate powers of transformation and creativity, emerging later as a female newly pregnant with inspiration.

In Ireland, St. Patrick's mission was to rid the land of its serpents; his intention being to deny women their power. The Christian Church also realized that while individuals were allowed to tap into their own unique potential from the energy running beneath their feet, religious leaders would never be able to control the masses. They renamed the underworld "the fires of hell," distorting the fact this is a *place of regeneration* ruled by the *Nordic goddess Hel*, and turning it into a *place of retribution:* hell.

It was during this time that the connection between the root chakra and the base chakra was essentially severed, prompting the serpent goddess kundalini to fall asleep. Even if we engage in spiritual or yogic practices that aim to awaken kundalini energy, we're only tapping into a fraction of the energy that is truly available to us when we reconnect to our root chakra and its fabulous dragon energy.

What Happens When We Embody Dragon Energy?

Perhaps I should add a warning at this stage of the handbook: ***Embodying dragon energy will change your life forever. Do not proceed beyond this point if you're fully content with your life as it is now!***

If you do decide to read further, **this is what you can expect when dragon energy enters your life:**

1. You'll probably encounter *spontaneous moments of joy,* which could last for hours on end.

2. You'll find yourself *happily letting go of limiting fears and unhealthy beliefs.*

3. You'll allow your dragon queen *to burn away anything in your life* which prevents you from being all that you are.

4. You'll know yourself as *a transformer,* offering everybody you meet the opportunity to change in your fiery cauldron (your womb).

5. *With your clear sight,* you'll be able to see beyond the masks of other people and be unimpressed by any ego pretense at being powerful, for *you* embody true power.

6. Because of the above, *you may be attacked emotionally* by those who don't want to be seen and don't want to change; they may even call you a witch or sorceress. *No problem!*

7. You'll be *less tolerant of people* who choose to stay in a rut, avoiding change at any cost.

8. You'll *opt to move away from people with dense* or low frequencies of energy.

9. *You'll feel empowered and fearless!*

Do you want to know my recommendation? Get in touch with your dragon energy today!

So how do you feel about inviting the dragon into your life today? Write your thoughts and feelings below:

CHAPTER 8

Rooting Ourselves into Love

Now that we have a sense of the huge potential awaiting us, the next step is to develop the roots that will become the pathways through which the dragon energy reaches our body and, at the same time, reconnect the base and root chakras, reuniting kundalini with her sister, the dragon queen.

Today I find that many people are ungrounded or unrooted into this planet, partly because they were never taught how important being grounded is for their spiritual growth and partly because of deeper emotional issues they may have. Given that our birth mother is synonymous with the Earth Mother, *if our relationship with our physical mother felt unsafe or threatening, it's often difficult to trust Mother Earth and even our own body,* causing us to live in our heads—trusting our thoughts, not our feelings.

In addition, with the root chakra abandoned so long ago, our sense of security and belonging commonly comes from the base chakra. The only problem is that the base chakra's idea of belonging is tribal, and to follow its dictates means that we have to follow many rules if we're going to avoid feelings of rejection, abandonment, and isolation. The stress many people feel today comes from attempts to abide by rules and values that don't allow for uniqueness of the individual. Only by rooting into the love and creative potential of Mother Earth will we understand the true nature of belonging.

This lack of connection to the planet is not a problem for some indigenous cultures who, when a baby is born, plant a tree over the buried placenta, symbolizing the "rooting" of the baby into Mother Earth. At puberty, another tree is planted a few feet from the original tree to create a doorway through which the child passes into adulthood. Such a practice guarantees that the child knows that their parents will guide and sustain them during their early years but that ultimately their sense of belonging and security will come from walking their own unique path, sustained by Mother Earth's food, wisdom, and creative energy that runs beneath their feet.

In the exercise that follows, I suggest you release the thoughts that *you don't deserve love* and surrender to Mother Earth's warm embrace, allowing her to nourish you without any preconditions and with loving support that will never smother you.

Welcome home!

Rooting Ourselves into Mother Earth
This exercise is perfect for whenever you feel stressed, ungrounded and a little lost in your head. Just by rooting yourself into Mother Earth you will find that you will have more energy, feel more relaxed and actually make better decisions.

- *You can do this exercise anywhere—in your office or at home— all you need is for your feet to be on the ground, so you do it standing or sitting.*

- *Close your eyes and take a few deep breaths, letting the in-breath last for the count of 3 and the out-breath last for the count of 6.*

- *As you breathe out, gather all the thoughts from your head and the stresses from your body and move them down through your feet into Mother Earth.*

- *Now, imagine on the soles of your feet are magnets and there's an even larger magnet in the center of Mother Earth and that magnet is pulling you into her.*

- *You find that you are actually not resisting it as it feels so good; you relax allowing yourself to enter into her loving space.*

- *Now see from the soles of your feet, roots going in all directions, some deep, some out to the side. And as those roots develop, you find that the beautiful moist soil of Mother Earth surrounds, loves and nurtures your roots.*

- *Mother Earth's energy loves without smothering. It holds and supports while allowing you to breathe and be yourself. Feel that pleasure of being loved and supported in such a nurturing way.*

- *Now just gently breathe some of that nourishment up through your roots, up through your legs and into your body.*

- *Very slowly, allow that beautiful love and nurturance to energize all the cells of your body.*

- *Then finally, move the energy into your mind and head, clearing out anything which does not serve you well at this moment.*

- *Bring love and pleasure into your whole body and mind.*

- *Finally, take your awareness back to your feet and back into the roots*

- *Now gently bring your awareness back to the room where you are, loosening up your feet very gently, shaking them out a little and in your own time open your eyes.*

Remember that as long as you're rooted, you will be in tune with yourself, with your own deep intention and with the joy that is yours to live in this moment.

Write about your experiences of Rooting Yourself into Mother Earth:

Filling Our Womb with Dragon Energy

Now we're ready to draw the golden water—dragon energy—into our womb, although it's important to remember we're dealing with a power that is volcanic in nature. It is not our servant and nor will it be possessed. So if we want to attract it into our body we need to persuade it to join us.

Here's an exercise to fill our womb with dragon energy:

a. *Send roots into Mother Earth, trusting her love as practiced above.*

b. *Focusing on the root chakra, feel the presence of a dynamic force flowing through this center.*

c. *Using the in-breath, slowly draw this golden energy up along your roots and legs, letting the energy fall back slightly on the out-breath.*

Since the dragon-serpent is attracted by rhythm, slowly swaying will enhance the spiraling ascension of this golden firewater.

d. *On reaching the vulva, imagine the energy passing along your vagina until it enters your womb or sacred temple.*

e. *Once inside the womb, imagine the dragon energy curling around its interior until the womb is full.*

f. *With dragon power now in your womb, insight becomes clearer and speech more powerful.*

g. *To complete the creation of the serpentine ladder, use the rhythm of your breath to spiral the dragon-serpent energy up through the remaining chakras, letting the in-breath last longer than the out-breath.*

h. *Finally, as the golden energy bursts through the crown chakra, allow it to shower down over your body, returning to Mother Earth to complete the circle.*

Write about your experiences of embodying your dragon power

This exercise is best performed standing, for your feet are rooted and your vagina is vertical in this position, offering easier access for the dragon energy to enter your sacred temple, the womb. In fact, all medi-ations for women should be carried out standing, squatting, or kneel-ing, for only then is the vagina in the correct position. The cross-legged approach illustrated below is definitely a male invention for it favors a part of their anatomy that acts like a 'stick' around which the serpent can spiral! You'll be surprised how many rituals are completely unsuitable for women but we continue to do them because we've been taught by a man!

I also want to send out a plea: Would you consider wearing skirts and dresses again rather than trousers and pants, as it allows for easier access of the dragon energy into your body? That's why priests, judges, and even Scottish men wear skirts or kilts, because they know that the source of their power is derived from Mother Earth. Of course, the energy can pass through the material of trousers, but when I'm wearing skirt, my femininity feels free and I can sway and wiggle my hips as much as I like!

CHAPTER 9

The Menstrual Cycle

Now that you've met your powerful inner dragon, let's look at how we can make space for it in our life so we can call upon it at any time we need help to get things done! Returning to the theme of three, there are three phases of our moon or menstrual cycle that follow the theme of the creative process, occurring, on average, every twenty-eight to twenty-nine days. The timing of the phases given below is based on this average duration of a menstrual cycle.

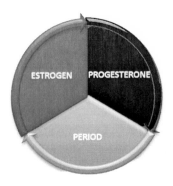

The Estrogen or Follicular Phase—Growth and Fertility

This phase, beginning after our period, sees us full of physical energy, clarity of thought, and enthusiasm. It's a great time to develop new ideas and projects, given that our mind is generally buzzing with plans.

This phase ends fourteen days after the start of our last period with the release of an idea/egg— known as **ovulation**. It's during the three days after ovulation (days 14–17) that we feel particularly sociable, confident, and sexually magnetic as we want to attract into our life, individuals who have the right spark to ignite or fertilize our dreams and ideas, so they may find full expression in the world.

If you want to conceive a baby, you'll be focused on finding the right partner during this time, so their sperm can unite with your egg, and you can begin the process of creating a beautiful baby together.

The Progesterone or Luteal Phase—Sharing and Nurturing

During days 15–18, we're often still keen to share our ideas with others. But eight to ten days before our next menstrual period, we find that our sociability is waning and we want to spend more time relaxing and being nurtured rather than taking care of everybody else.

When asked to take on new projects, it's best to decline if possible during this phase, as we're typically more creative and efficient *after* our period. If we don't rest, refuel, and otherwise take care of ourselves, we're more likely to experience the uncomfortable symptoms of premenstrual syndrome (PMS).

One to two days before our period, it's important to make space for time alone, when we can reflect on the month that's ending and decide: *What wisdom will I take from this month and what am I going to release during my period?*

The Period, Menses, or Moon-Time—Release and Inspiration

This phase, lasting anywhere from three to seven days, is the most powerful time for a woman, for now she releases her hold on outdated energy and happily reconnects to the Great Mother's source of eternal wisdom to receive inspiration for the new month!

Menopause and Beyond

When we reach menopause, hormonal changes cause our periods to cease. Our postmenopausal body is now programmed to cycle directly with the moon.

- **The waxing moon** equates to the estrogen phase

- **The waning moon** equates to the progesterone phase

- **The dark moon** equates to the moon-time or period

Unfortunately, many women lose interest in their rhythm once they reach menopause or after a hysterectomy. Yet it's so important to our well-being to set time aside around the dark moon to clear our bodies, reconnect to the mystery of the Great Mother, and be inspired. Symptoms such as diarrhea, vomiting, urinary infection, rashes, or sinus discharge are all ways the body uses to attempt to clear out old energies when there's no longer a menstrual bleed. By following the rhythm of the three-day moon ritual (detailed later) your body will be so grateful!

Whatever our age, when we stay in rhythm with our cycles,
we experience well-being and balance in our lives.

However, when we attempt to live a 24/7 life of sameness,
we're asking for trouble!

CHAPTER 10

PMS: Premenstrual Syndrome

Many people joke about PMS or *that time of the month,* but if you're the woman suffering, it's no laughing matter. One minute you're yelling at your partner and the next, crying into your favorite ice cream, just wanting to be hugged. Affecting 60 percent of women, PMS causes varying degrees of distress through a myriad of symptoms, which include breast tenderness, weight gain, headache, bloating, constipation, fatigue, irrational anger, mood swings, low libido, depression, and sugar cravings.

Today many women are multitasking—trying to balance work, home, friends, and family, with some "me" time. This commonly results in women being actively occupied for many more hours than their male colleagues. Fearful of being seen as weak or inadequate, we push ourselves to keep up with the masculine rhythm that is pretty steady throughout the month.

But the female mind and body are carefully programmed to follow a cyclical, not linear, pattern, designed to maintain optimal levels of creativity. When we fail to do this, our system becomes distressed.

So is it possible to pay equal attention to the different phases of our cycle in the midst of our busy lives? The estrogen phase is fairly easy as it represents creative activity leading to an outward expression of adrenaline-motivated "doing." This phase fits in very nicely with society's expectations of success and productivity, reflected by the commonly asked question: *What have you been doing today?*

But after ovulation we start to run into problems. For now, progesterone—the nurturing hormone—teams up with the relaxing parasympathetic nervous system and together they cause us to want to withdraw, refuel, and relax—activities that are often considered self-indulgent and nonproductive.

When I worked as a homeopath, the commonest remedies used for PMS were *Sepia* and *Lachesis*, which perfectly describe how women feel a week before their period. Sepia is the ink of the cuttlefish, produced when it *just wants to be left alone*. Lachesis is snake venom, released when the snake *feels trapped in a corner*. Without a healthy balance between activity and rest, our body and mind become distressed and our level of creativity will decline. Of course, we can't avoid work during our progesterone phase but we can create space for pampering and relaxation, leading to a happier mind and body.

Here Are Some More Suggestions for the Seven Days Prior to Your Period

1. **Place yourself at the top of your priority list:** Let everybody know you're not going to be so available to meet their needs during this time.

2. **Ask for help** rather than saying: *I'm fine, I'll do it myself.*

3. **Don't take on any new projects** until after your period.

4. **Arrange some pleasurable and nurturing pastimes**: If you feel you "should" do something, don't do it.

5. **Avoid foods that are stimulants** including sweets, caffeine, and alcohol.

6. **Set aside precious time to be alone** so you can reflect on life and decide what's working for you and what's not. Be ready to release old emotions and unrealistic dreams during your menstrual period.

PMS is not an illness; it's a distress call from our inner woman urging us to return to our natural, nurturing rhythm.

CHAPTER 11

The Power of Our Periods

I wish I'd known then what I know now about my menstrual cycle; life would have been so much easier! My mother always called her periods "the curse." Now I see them as less of a curse and much more of a blessing. I love the name "moon-time," which continually reminds me of my connection to the cyclical nature of the moon, even beyond menopause.

With the erroneous belief still circulating that the only reason that we have a menstrual cycle is so that we may get pregnant, many girls today are being persuaded to see their periods as *an unnecessary inconvenience,* and use pills, patches, or injections to delay or suppress them.

However, This Would Be a Mistake,

Given That the Most Powerful and Creative Times in a Woman's Life Occur during Her Period

The Red Tent movement, inspired by the book of the same name by Anita Diamant, has done much to draw women's attention to the importance of the moon-time—a time when women come together in a sacred place to share stories, laugh, be nurtured, and learn about blood mysteries. This is a great start, but there's still a long way to go! I hope to be able to persuade you that if we don't honor our periods or the postmenopausal dark moon ritual each month, the evolution of humanity will start to slow down and will eventually become stagnant.

Together, let's make sure that never happens!

To Recap, the Menstrual Cycle Has Three Phases Occurring every Twenty-Eight to Twenty-Nine Days

1. **The period, menses, or moon-time**, when we release the old and make way for new inspiration.

2. **The estrogen or follicular phase**, linked to the development of the egg/idea until its release at ovulation, awaiting fertilization.

3. **The progesterone or luteal phase**, linked to sharing, nurturing, and self-reflection.

As you see, I've now placed the menstrual period at the beginning of the creative cycle, because its role is the most important of the three phases.

So, if these are or were the most powerful days of your month, how do you or did you relate to your period, menses or moon-time?

1. *What do you or did you like about having periods?*

2. *What 3 adjectives come to mind when you think about your periods?*

3. *What age did you experience your first period? Was it celebrated? If so how?*

4. *Who taught you about your menstrual cycle?*

5. *Do you honor and celebrate your periods or lunar cycle today?*

6. *Do you or did you talk with girlfriends about your periods?*

7. *What moon-time products do you or did you use in the early years of your menstrual history? And now what do you use, if you still bleed?*

8. *Do you or did you have problems with your periods or PMS?*

9. *If yes, did anybody ever try to help you understand the deeper reason?*

10. *What would you like to tell a young girl today about her periods and menstrual cycle?*

Clearing Away the Clutter

Imagine the womb as a beautiful bowl, vase or vessel waiting to be filled with new creative energy and inspiration. Located at the base of the bowl is a brilliant glow representing your heart or soul's light. Every time you empty your bowl, you reconnect to this light, your soul's purpose and, in turn, to the Great Mother's love. In essence, the main role of our period is to clear away the clutter that prevents us from creating a life which fully expresses the unique and exquisite being that we are.

Iranian bronze bowl (from Los Angeles County Museum of Art)

To allow the light to shine, we must empty our bowl of anything which keeps us from connecting to our soul's love which includes old emotions, wounds, stories, outdated beliefs, unattainable dreams, unhealthy relationships, unrealistic expectations, and even positive memories, for they all can keep us locked into the past.

For the sake of our children, we must stop creating our future from old wounds

Such energies have been gathering in our womb over many years, usually without adequate release, because nobody told us that this is the purpose of our periods. The elements of earth and water are only too happy to receive and cleanse us of our clutter, so we may reconnect to the mystery and spiritual potential radiating from our soul's light.

CHAPTER 12

Rites of Passage: The First Period

So maybe someone you know is about to transition from childhood to womanhood? Congratulations! I'm going to write this as if you're the mother of the girl making this transition (although, of course, if you're a close friend or a female relative, you may carry out the same preparations and celebrations on the girl's behalf).

This rite of passage—*menarche*—means as much to the mother as it does to the daughter, for it reflects a change in their relationship as together they embody the women's blood mysteries, sharing intimacies as never before.

A girl's first period usually appears about two years after the start of puberty, with its blossoming breasts and the growth of body hair. Menarche can occur anywhere from eight to sixteen years of age, although commonly it begins between eleven and fourteen. Although it's impossible to know the actual date of menarche before it appears, a young girl is usually psychologically ready from nine to ten years onward to understand the responsibilities of womanhood. I hope these responsibilities will be expanded beyond the usual roles of cooking, cleaning, and taking care of babies, and embrace the teachings of women's mysteries that are shared in this handbook!

In indigenous cultures, the preparation time before menarche is as important as the celebration that surrounds the first period. In preparation for your own daughter's first period, it would be wonderful if you, as her mother, could spend some time creating a journal or photo album of all the special moments you've shared with your daughter—spanning your pregnancy, her birth, and continuing on through the years. The aim is to remind our daughters of the strong bond we've shared and continue to share with them. It's lovely if female relatives and friends wish to contribute their memories as well.

Puberty's onset a few years before menarche gives us ample opportunity to create special moments for girl-only outings designed to enhance the fun of being a woman. At this age, your daughter will be very mindful of how you embrace your femininity and how you feel about your periods and female body. What you share and how you behave is up to you but remember—you're her primary role model!

Preparation

1. Let your daughter decide on a toy, piece of clothing, or other object that was important to her as a child but that now, on becoming a woman, she's *ready to give to a younger child.*

2. Talk about *role models* with her and let her share with you the qualities she admires in women she knows.

3. Teach her *how to root* herself in Mother Earth so she'll always be able to return here to renew her energy and creativity.

4. Teach her how to *lean back into the heart of her soul* so that she can hear her intuition.

5. Together *buy or make a dress* that she'll wear when her period starts, along with any suitable jewelry.

6. Create a *family tree of her female ancestors,* so she knows where she's come from and can recite the names of these women going back at least the last three generations.

7. Let her meet her *doorkeepers of her sacred temple* (more on this in chapter 18).

8. Teach her the *three phases of the moon-time ritual,* (see chapter 16) which you can start to practice together at the time of the dark moon until her cycle begins.

9. Let your daughter appreciate that *her menstrual blood* is her special connection with all females, including the Earth Mother. There are several ways to collect and release the blood during menses each suitable for different women and different flow levels. Have fun exploring them together!

Celebrating the Menarche within a Woman's Circle

1. Create a *guest list* in advance of adolescent girlfriends and female friends and relatives who you and your daughter can trust to create a safe and sacred space for the celebrations. Call them into circle as soon as possible after your daughter's first period begins.

2. Some cultures include men, such as the father, in the celebrations, although the ceremony itself should *only include women.* It's a lovely idea for the father to give a present or flowers to his daughter but even in today's culture, a daughter can be embarrassed by her father knowing too much about her personal details.

3. If possible, *create a setting* that imitates a red tent and ask all the women to enter it and sit in circle. In the initial part of the ceremony, your daughter will wear the clothes of her girlhood.

4. It's important to create a spiral of feminine energy by calling in the ancestors. Your daughter should start by saying: *I am ... daughter of ... granddaughter of....* Sisters and aunts may also be included in her list.

5. Each woman should *introduce herself* in the same manner and share her stories about her own first period.

6. The next step is for each woman to share something she's choosing to release that month. Your daughter will be last, stating: *I release my childhood.*

7. At this point, your daughter will *change her clothes*, dressing herself in her new clothes and jewelry.

8. In ancient times, the women would take this young woman *to a pool of water* where they would help to remove her clothes and bathe her all over, washing away girlhood and celebrating her beautiful blossoming woman's body. Through their touch they would teach her to enjoy the sensuality of her body without shame. Then she would be dressed in her new clothes. Sadly, in many cultures, loving touch between women has been lost or denigrated, adding to the shame many women feel toward their bodies today.

9. Now it's time for *celebration and connection*, sharing food, sisterhood and laughter!

10. The final stage of initiation begins with each woman presenting *a gift to your daughter*—whether it's something physical, a poem, or words of wisdom—to represent her induction into the sacred mysteries.

11. The *last word is reserved for your daughter*, wherein she can speak of what it means to her to have reached womanhood, share her commitment to embody the mysteries, and honor you by becoming a strong and beautiful woman.

There are variations to this celebration depending on the culture involved. In the Japanese culture, special red rice and beans, in a dish called *Sekihan*, is served at the meal, while in the Navajo tradition the girl makes cornmeal pudding for the tribe to taste and wears clothes to the imitate the goddess known as Changing Woman. Many tribes build a moon hut for their young woman, to be used during her moontime, where she can receive teachings from the wise women. The huts are commonly located near water, which acknowledges the power of water to dissolve away separation and allow a full connection to the Great Mother.

CHAPTER 13

Deepening the Mystery

Imagine that every month, you have the chance to lay aside all the concerns of the outer world and immerse yourself in three days of nurturing, laughter and pleasure with your favorite girlfriends in a sacred space where anything can be shared, without the fear of being judged, shamed or rejected. This is what awaits you when you realign to the rhythm of your body and reconnect to the mysteries of the menstrual period or dark moon days. Realistically, we can't step away from everything but when we connect and commit to this innate female yearning, our enhanced sense of wellbeing will encourage us to continue the practice. It's time to go deeper!

The Three Phases of a Female's Moon-Time

Within the female's menstrual period or moon-time there are three distinct phases that formed the core of the Greek Eleusinian Mysteries. These phases or steps include:

1. Clearing and emptying; **release**

2. Nurturing and merging; **connection**

3. Filling ourselves with creative energy; **inspiration**

As you'll notice, these phases mirror aspects of the monthly cycle, but now are magnified into just three days, leading us deeper into the mysteries.

Let's look at each of these phases in turn:

RELEASE: Phase 1

At least one day of the month, every woman (whatever our age) is given the chance to empty our bowl—the uterus—of everything we have collected that defines us in the outer world and return to the mysterious realms of creative potential. It is this ability 'to die' to our outer identity and expectations of the outer world every month that probably led to the suppression of women's mysteries by the patriarchy, because without a fear of death, how can they control the masses?

> **So what is the mark of a powerful woman?** *Her willingness to become empty*!

This may sound daunting but it's actually as easy as breathing. *Here's a simple exercise:*

During your next in-breath, imagine filling yourself with creative energy until you radiate this abundant energy at the top of the breath. Then, reverse the process, breathing out, expiring, until you're completely empty and can rest for a moment in the vast ocean of possibilities which awaits your attention. On your next in-breath, imagine drawing into yourself some of that creative energy and repeat the process three times.

You'll soon discover that the greater the depth of the out-breath, the greater capacity you have for an in-breath; the greater the emptiness, the greater capacity for fullness and abundance. The same is true for our bowl/ uterus; when our bowl is only partially empty, there is little room for new inspiration.

The questions to ask are these:

1. *What beliefs, stories etc. stop me embodying my unique and beautiful inner woman?*

2. *Where do I hold myself separate or disconnected from other women?*

3. *Do I believe I deserve to be embraced by the love of my inner light or soul?*

Deciding what needs to be released is part of the preparation stage that we'll cover in the next chapter.

CONNECTION; Phase 2

Our moon-time should be one of the most joyful times for a woman! Not only do we get the chance to connect to our inner light and other women but also to the spirit, love, and wisdom of all women, past, present and future and ultimately with the Great Mother. A desire for this loving union is an essential part of the blood or scarlet-water mysteries, which is why women have always gathered around water—wells, lakes, rivers, and oceans—for water is the medicine of women, dissolving away anything which keeps us separate from our true self and the togetherness of womanhood. We choose to enter the water not because we are unclean but to set our spirit free.

As a fetus, we grow and are nurtured in the ethereal waters of our mother's womb and joyfully reconnect to this mystery and eternal love through our own womb's scarlet waters during our moon-time. As our blood collects in our womb, it gathers within itself anything that keeps us separate from knowing ourselves fully.

Our determination to connect to divine love is similar to a drop of water that flows through streams and rivers to reach the mighty ocean. On becoming part of the ocean, we find that although we lose our individual identity, we're embraced by universal love and wisdom; we become everything and everything is us.

Balancing our Masculine and Feminine

To understand the relationship between separation and connection it may help to look at the balance between our masculine and feminine selves. The role of our masculine self on Earth is to take ideas and, through planning and activity, bring them into reality. This manifested expression defines us and gives us an identity: *I am . . . this is what I do . . . this is my story. . . .* We have created a separate ego-identity that radiates self-confidence, much as the full moon shines out in the night sky.

But, like the light of the moon which starts to wane, once we have manifested our dreams, we need to turn our attention inward to gather new ideas from the source of creation, the Great Mother. Having nurtured ourselves with our experiences, it's time to slowly dissolve the ego-identity and follow our feminine self—the soul—into mystery, for only here can we tap into the fullness of our potential.

Just as our in-breath and out-breath need to work together in harmony, so do our masculine and feminine aspects. Unfortunately, since the essence of what it is to be a woman has been forgotten over time, many women have perfected their masculine ego-identity but have lost touch with the feminine realms of creative mystery. When challenged to empty the bowl and find their feminine nature, they use questions, excuses, and intellect to ensure that their defenses are never breached. 64

Our masculine self uses the mind—stored with information from previous experiences—to create its reality; a recipe for stagnation. Our feminine self trusts the love of the intuitive heart to enter the unknown and float on the ocean of possibilities, embraced by the love of the Divine Mother.

INSPIRATION: Phase 3

For too long, we've been taught that divine inspiration comes from above our heads, and that wisdom was something to be handed down from the minds of wise elders. And yet, wisdom doesn't belong to the mind but comes from a knowingness stored within Mother Earth, accessed by our intuitive heart. You may remember times when you've said: *I can't explain why but I just know this to be true.*

Our modern obsession with linear time, where there is a past and future, has blinded us to the fact that all creation is already energetically in place, just waiting to be manifest. This is the wisdom of feminine circles and cycles, not of masculine straight lines. But through clever patriarchal propaganda, many of us still look skyward for inspiration, never questioning or contemplating the wise dragon blueprint that runs beneath our feet.

In truth, this amazing fluidic creative grid or matrix of potentiality flowing within Mother Earth was downloaded into the planet millions of years ago and is constantly revealing different parts of its mystery as our consciousness evolves and we dream the matrix alive. The ancient people knew of the grid's presence and would sing as they walked along certain paths, singing into existence a new dream or frequency of consciousness, just as the song of the whales sends new frequencies of awareness into our oceans.

To act as vessels for the birth of new ideas, our ancestors also built female-shaped stone monuments over the places where the dragon lines crossed. Now it's our turn to be sacred vessels of transformation, sending our roots into the Earth and attracting into ourselves dragon energy full of rich potential.

The more we empty and connect, the deeper we're able to tap into the creative matrix and draw into ourselves a dream waiting to be born; our spiritual destiny. This dream, dissolved within the golden dragon energy, enters our body and is carried up along our serpentine ladder, until a chalice or cup is created above our head. Since our energy is powerfully magnetic, our chalice will naturally attract into it a spark or seed of inspiration, which ignites the dream we're carrying in our body—*a virgin birth.*

To help deepen this understanding, here's an analogy. Let's imagine that the energetic blueprint or dream you've drawn into your body is that of an *oak tree*. The energetic soil of your awareness then says: *I'm ready to give birth to an oak tree.* As you hold your chalice aloft, you'll naturally attract into it an *acorn* that acts as a spark of inspiration, turning a dream into a mighty oak tree.

Release, Connect, and Inspire: These three phases are the essence of the three-day ritual that I'd love to see all women practice, whatever our age, either on the first three days of the period or on the three days of the dark moon, if we no longer bleed.

But first we must prepare!

CHAPTER 14

Reflection and Preparation

Preparation

In ancient Eleusis a time of preparation was always required before anyone was allowed to enter the inner sanctum or womb of the Great Mother where the actual mysteries took place. During this time, participants would be asked certain questions to see if they were truly ready to release their hold on their outer identity, connect to the ocean of possibilities, and become inspired.

Letting go is never easy, especially when we've devoted so much time and effort to create our perfect persona. But for these ancient participants, this event was the pinnacle of their year when they could take time from their busy lives to connect with powers and dreams which opened their world to a new sense of freedom, fulfillment and delight.

Even though, we're not able to transport ourselves to ancient Greece, here are some questions to ask yourself one to two days before your period or before the start of the dark moon, which will begin the process of release, connection and inspiration. *You can write your answers below but perhaps use a pencil, so you change the answers each month.*

1. Celebration

Remember I mentioned that the deeper our emptiness, the more we can fill with inspiration? Well, the reverse is also true: the fuller we are of ourselves—self-confident—the easier it is to become empty. How do we achieve this? By doing a little dance or singing a song in celebration of our achievements. This may sound childish, but we adults could learn a lot from two- and three-year-olds; they love showing off what they have done!

Without celebration, life becomes one long project without any satisfaction. The reason many people fear death and loss is because they've never felt fully alive. So in preparation, please write a list of three things you're celebrating or three things about yourself that make you proud this month and, as you read them back to yourself, dance a little gig!

Ask yourself: What Three Achievements or Successes am I Celebrating this Month? As you write them down, give yourself a hug or do a little gig!

2. Embracing the Gems of Wisdom

Another way to boost our ego or self-confidence is by gleaning gems of wisdom from every single experience. If we're unwilling to take any responsibility for events in our life, preferring to believe that life *happens to* us, then we become life's victim rather than its creator. What if I told you that you're a highly evolved soul who carefully mapped out your life before coming to Earth to achieve your greatest spiritual growth? When viewed in this way, every experience offers a gift or gem of wisdom that you can take to your heart—building confidence, respect, and inner strength.

So what Gems of Wisdom Am I Ready to Accept into My Heart?

   a. *What did I learn about myself this month?*

   b. *What strengths and talents emerged this month that I want to use again?*

   c. *Did I meet a part of myself—a sub-personality—that, even though I might not like its behavior, is still a part of me? Can I accept it into my heart?*

   d. *What wisdom will I take from my experiences?*

3. Grieving into Emptiness

Commonly cluttering our wombs are partially degraded stories, relationships, and unrealistic dreams. We had planned to let them go, but have difficulty with that final push because if we let go of our stories: *Who are we?*

They are part of our ego-identity. We're stuck in the grieving process that, although usually only associated with death of a loved one, is actually our psyche's way of helping us transition from one state of reality to the next one, making space in our womb for new inspiration. It can be likened to the cocoon stage between the caterpillar and butterfly, with seven recognizable stages:

1. Numbness

2. Denial

3. Anger at others

4. Blaming and shaming of ourselves

5. Bargaining and praying

6. Confusion and depression

7. Acceptance and moving forward

Every time something doesn't work out the way we want or something ends, we pass through these steps. Unfortunately, we also have a tendency to get stuck along the way—bottling up anger, resentment, or guilt rather than accepting the truth: *It's over.*

While these old stories and painful emotions remain in our bowl, we will continually create our reality based on our past wounds, wondering why we keep suffering hurt and disappointment over and over again. Every encounter has a purpose for our soul; if we're having difficulty letting go of old emotions, it's because we haven't yet deciphered the lesson and wisdom we're meant to take from the experience. Sometimes we just cling to a situation, however suffocating, because we're scared of the freedom and power awaiting us when we stop playing small.

The process of grief naturally takes up to three years. After that time, the story of loss and the accompanying feelings start to clutter our uterus. If you still hold emotions about an event that happened more than three years ago, you're stuck in the grieving process. In this case, it's time to empty the bowl and allow new creative dragon energy into your life!

So what are you ready to Release this Month? You don't have to release everything in one month. Some of the questions will be more relevant depending on what's happening in your life from month to month. Be gentle but commit to repeating this practice every month for the rest of your life!

a. *Where am I living in a delusion or fantasy and not facing the truth?*

b. *Where am I playing small or limiting my abilities?*

c. *Where am I trying to revive something, like a relationship, which is finished?*

d. *What expectations do I have of myself or others that are unrealistic?*

e. *Where am I holding onto anger, frustration, or resentment, which is now only hurting me?*

f. *Where am I still blaming and shaming myself for something that was outside of my control?*

g. *Where am I bargaining with "God" through prayers and entreaties to make something happen the way I want it to? Can I stop being so self-willed and trust my soul to show me the way?*

h. *Can I trust that I'm loved and things will work out, but not always the way I envisioned?*

i. *Can I accept that confusion, fatigue, and depression are not necessarily signs of illness, but are healthy signs that I am, at last, letting go of control and am ready to surrender into mystery?*

Once you've made your list of your celebrations, gems, and what you're ready to release, take it to the beginning of the three-day ritual which begins on the evening of the first day of your period or the day before the new moon if you are post-menopausal. I'll give you more details of the ritual very soon. If you no longer bleed, *fill a glass with water and surround the vessel with your hands.* Speaking aloud, infuse the water with everything you're ready to release, carefully keeping the glass in a safe place, to be used at the start of ritual.

4. In Service to the Family

Apart from their own clearing, our female ancestors also assisted the family in clearing *their* energy during the moon-time. A few days before a woman's period, our ancestral sister would gather her family around her—especially the men—and would ask each in turn whether there were any old emotions or beliefs they wanted her to release during her period. She would agree to take on these energies as long as the men and other family members could answer this question: "*How have you grown in wisdom from this experience?*"

If she was satisfied with the answers given, she'd take the emotions into her womb and turn them into blood. If she wasn't satisfied with the answers, she would tell them to come back the following month. The family members knew how important this service was to their spiritual growth and therefore were only too willing to comply. As well, they were very happy to serve and nurture their women during their moon-time!

5. Letting Go of the Ego

Our ego-identity is the masculine part of the self that creates thoughts and stories so we can know who we are and feel safe. It doesn't care if the beliefs about ourselves nurture us as long as they define us. This means that if we believe *we're unlovable* or *don't deserve to be happy,* that's what we will keep creating in our life. But once a month, we're given a chance to face these beliefs and ask: *Do these beliefs bring me pleasure and kindness?* If they don't, let's add them to our list to be released.

Sometimes we "talk" about doing something but never plant the seed to allow the dream to blossom, fearful of facing the emptiness that comes when we see our dreams manifest.

Facing true emptiness of the ego can be challenging, especially if we've never made contact with the loving light of our soul. Sometimes it takes a crisis to look for this light, given that it's always easier to see the light of a candle in darkness than in broad daylight.

Rather than becoming overwhelmed by the idea of losing everything and finding no light and love at the base of your bowl, I suggest you proceed in stages:

- *Start with the practice of leaning back into the arms of your soul while sitting or lying on your back. By doing this you will sense your heart resonating with the pulse of your soul.*

- *Spend time in nature every day enjoying nature's sensual beauty and unconditional love.*

- *Be around pets or those who bring you joy and comfort.*

- *This will help to open the heart to the idea of being loved.*

Here are some more questions to encourage you to slowly release your grip on your ego-identity and trust the loving embrace of the Great Mother:

a. *What are three ways in which I define myself in the world today? I am . . .*

b. *Do I believe there's a part of me which exists beyond these identities?*

c. *Am I addicted to certain habits; such as working, being busy, answering e-mails, blogging, posting on Facebook or helping others? Could I live without doing these things for three days?*

d. *Where am I over-identified with my "stories" or wounds from the past? Am I ready to know myself beyond these stories?*

e. *What beliefs about myself, fill my mind with monkey chatter but never nurture my soul?*

f. *Where am I hiding from connecting with my true self within a spiritual, new age or religious belief or dogma? What if nothing I believe is true?*

g. *Which of my relationships hold a strong emotional tie? Could I release that tie one day a month to allow freedom for both parties?*

h. *What do I fear losing the most? Can I surrender to love and know that, no matter the outcome, everything will be all right?*

Take one question at a time and, when answering it, be kind to and honest with yourself. No rush, no pressure. Just imagine, on every out-breath, releasing all of your beliefs so that—just for a moment—you may experience the joy of expansive love and open-ended possibilities.

CHAPTER 15

Honoring Our Moon-Time

In honor of the sacred nature of our periods and the dark moon days, an indigenous woman would set aside sacred space and time for the three-day moon ritual.

1. **During her period or the dark moon she would enter a moon lodge or red tent, which was usually located near water.** Here she'd meet with other women who were also on their moon-time, spending the days sharing stories, laughing, crying, napping, crafting, and resting. Even though, in today's modern world, taking time away from family and work may not be all that practical, it's lovely to set aside sacred space in the day to catch up on reading, enjoy creative projects, or just for self-nurturing!

2. **No indigenous woman would prepare food** for the family during these days. This is because at this point, the woman's body contains the emotions and beliefs her family has asked her to discard; touching the food will mean that they are ingesting the unwanted energy again. Let your family cook and take care of *you* for a change! If you live with other women whose cycle is different from yours, it's fun to cook for each other during these powerful days.

3. **It's unwise to have sex** with a man on these days, as you can actually decrease his energy, for you are in a powerful

transformative state of being. For the same reason it's best to limit physical contact with men as much as possible during this time.

4. **It's also unwise for a woman to take part in any sacred ceremony** except with other women on their moon-time because her powerful energy has been known to break objects.

When we follow these suggestions in respect and honor of our cycles, we'll see many wonderful changes in our lives, including a lessening of any symptoms linked to our period.

What plans are you going to put in place to ensure you honor your period (if you still bleed) or your dark moon days:

Are Menstrual Cramps, Cramping your Style? Primary Dysmenorrhea

Recently I was surprised to hear how many girls aged fifteen had already been put on the pill or another hormone treatment because of menstrual cramps, without trying any other type of treatment or looking for an underlying cause.

Fifty percent of girls and women complain of pain just before or during the first few days of their period, and 10 percent of these women are distressed enough to need to take time away from school or work. The cramping pain is more commonly in the lower abdomen but may also appear as a dull ache in the lower back and thighs. It can be linked to headaches, nausea, dizziness, and fainting. It's believed to be caused by a number of factors, including an imbalance between estrogen and progesterone levels (similar to PMS), increased levels of the pain-producing prostaglandins, and a constriction of the blood vessels feeding the uterus.

Exercise, hot-water bottles, mild anti-inflammatory tablets, and the pill have been the treatments of choice in the past. But I'd love to see the results when girls and women start to accept and work with their powerful dragon energy (detailed in chapter 7), both to clear their uterus at the start of their period and to fill it with energy at the end. I believe that fear of such power contributes to the onset of menstrual cramps.

CHAPTER 16

The Three-Day Moon Ritual in Detail

Day 1: Release—*First day of your period or first day of the dark moon*

At sunset, standing on Mother Earth, hold your prepared lists of celebrations, gems, and those things to be released which, if you no longer bleed, have already been dissolved into a glassful of water during preparation. It's good to stand on natural earth rather than concrete, and with bare feet if possible.

1. **Move your awareness into your heart chakra** and, placing your hand on this center, read from the list of celebrations and then the list of gems saying:

   This month I'm celebrating . . . name what you're celebrating

   I accept into my heart this wisdom and what I've learned about myself . . . name this

   I accept into my heart this part of myself (sub-personality) . . . name it . . . *but will no longer let it control my life.*

2. **Bending your knees slightly or squatting, say:**

   a. *Great Mother Earth I connect to you through the blood mysteries.*

   b. Read out your list of those things you're ready to release.

c. If you're bleeding, imagine shedding some blood onto the Earth or if you're not bleeding, pour the water from your glass onto Mother Earth. If you're in a private setting, it's perfectly acceptable to actually bleed directly onto the Earth.

d. Then say: *I ask you to receive and transform these thoughts and emotions, with gratitude.*

e. Finally state: *I am empty and connect to your great mystery.*

f. Then send your roots into Mother Earth and feel yourself being received and held by her love.

g. Once united to the mystery beneath your feet, find somewhere to lie down, such as a bed, a bath or even the earth. Imagine floating or bobbing on an ocean of love where you connect to the eternal compassion and wisdom of all women. When go to sleep that night, say to yourself: *Job well done!*

Day 2: **Connection**—*second day of your period or second day of the dark moon (day of the new moon)*

This is a day for rest, pleasure, and self-nurturing. Continue the theme of connection from last night and if it's not possible to share this day with girlfriends or loving women, such as in a Red Tent, take time in the day to imagine being in a sacred space where laughter, tears, dreams and nurturing are shared with sisters of the womb, heart and soul, whether from this world or from the realm of spirit.

Day 3: **Inspiration**—*third day of your period or third day of the dark moon*

a. *Before the busyness of the day begins, find a quiet place to meditate, making sure your feet are on the ground.*

b. *Take your awareness to your heart chakra, the seat of your soul, and ask:* **Guide me in the way of fullness, fertility, and joy.**

c. *Send your roots into Mother Earth, focusing particularly on your root chakra through which the dragon matrix of potentiality flows.*

d. *As you breathe in, draw into your body the blueprint of the dream you're going to birth this month, dissolved in golden dragon energy. Don't think about what you want but allow your soul to choose.*

e. *Allow the rich creative energy to spiral up along your roots, legs, and through your vagina into your womb.*

f. *As the dragon energy passes up through your body bringing new life, it also continues to burn away anything which keeps you separate from your full power and purpose.*

g. *When your womb is full, if you're premenopausal, send the dragon energy out to your ovaries, stimulating one of the eggs to start to develop in resonance with the incoming dream.   Then let this rich creative energy, containing the new dream, continue its journey up through the chakras, along the serpentine ladder, until it reaches the heart and say: I'm ready to live my soul's full purpose this life;* **I embrace healing, joy, fulfillment, and abundance.**

h. *Allow the dream-filled dragon energy to continue upward until it fills the beautiful serpentine chalice above your head, at the crown chakra. Since dragon energy is highly magnetic, it will pull towards itself the perfect seed or spark of inspiration to ignite your potential, turning a dream into reality.*

i. *At this point, it's a good idea to hum—like a bee—for this sound eases the opening of doors into the multidimensional realms of consciousness where these seeds exist.*

j. *Sometimes such seeds or sparks appear as symbols or colors, or we may sense energy that gives us insights into the dream we're manifesting this month. But it's not important to intellectually know; it's much better to stay in the mystery and trust our heart and soul.*

k. *Now empty the fertilized dream from the chalice into the heart and from the heart into the womb, planting it into Mother Earth at the root chakra.*

l. *Keep a note of insights received during this meditation and any others that cross your mind during the day. At the end of the day, say:* **I'm committed to birthing my new ideas and to embracing the changes this will bring to my life.** *Let new creativity flow over the next 14 days.*

In an ideal world, on the fourth day we would share our insights with our family and male colleagues and they would go away to bring our ideas into existence through practical masculine abilities while we, as a female spiritual leader, would hold the vision.

But today, with Superwoman in control, we often find ourselves doing everything while wondering: *Where is there a man to help me*? The reality is that when women embody their feminine gifts, it will give our men the encouragement and space to do what they do best and everybody will be happy.

CHAPTER 17

Baskets Full of Eggs

Now that we know our bodies are beautifully designed to give birth every month—not only to babies but also to new ideas—it's time to explore the source of this creativity. We need to go no further than our ovaries, which at birth are packed with *2 million eggs or oocytes*, each containing a unique piece of our spiritual potential. In other words, there are *2 million possible dreams or ideas* waiting for you to claim, nurture, and birth. As a woman, our greatest pleasure and power comes from developing, cherishing, and expressing these creative gems—babies or ideas—every month, and sharing them first with our family and then with the world!

Women are the soil for all new birth.

There's just one little problem. During the first nine months of life, as we lie in the womb, our beautiful pristine eggs are *marinated in the emotional soup of our mother.* To make matters worse, her eggs were marinated in her mother's womb and so it continues right down the line. Everything our mother feels and believes is slowly absorbed into our eggs so that, by the time we are born, our dreams and ideas are already tainted by her experiences and by those of our maternal mothers passing back through the generations. That's why it's so important, before you choose to become pregnant, to take time to *"clear and prepare the soil,"* (as described earlier) emptying your psyche of unhealthy beliefs, outdated stories, and old emotions. This will give your children, especially your daughters, the best chance of living a fulfilling and creative life.

What was going on in your mother's life during and even before she was pregnant with you? Here are some questions to consider:

a. *Was your pregnancy planned?*

b. *What were your mother's thoughts about being a mother?*

c. *Had your mother ever lost a child or had a miscarriage before you were conceived?*

d. *Had your mother had a good relationship with her mother?*

Disharmony of the Ovaries

If we accept that illness occurs as a result of a combination of factors, it's important to look at the physical, emotional, and spiritual environments that surround the woman and her illness; only then can we begin a self-care program which may be utilized in conjunction with any allopathic or complementary treatment.

With our ovaries as the source of creativity, any illness in this area may suggest that the flow of creativity has become blocked or that we've been silenced, closing down our ability to share our ideas. Ovaries also represent our femininity, which may have been damaged by messages we received in childhood or from our ancestors.

Here Are Some Questions to Ask Yourself If Your Ovaries Are Distressed

1. *Has anything happened in your life recently that has affected your self-confidence as a woman?*

2. *How easy is it for you to express your ideas and dreams?*

3. *Do you feel free to live your dreams or are there too many obstacles?*

4. *Did anybody ever tell you that, as a woman, you have nothing to offer?*

5. *What do you do on a weekly basis that gives you the chance to be creative, such as writing, painting, dancing, singing, or cooking, for example?*

Polycystic Ovary Syndrome (PCOS)

As a young gynecology doctor, I saw very few cases of PCOS; today one in fifteen women are affected and polycystic ovary syndrome has become one of the major causes of infertility and irregular periods.

What Do We Know?

1. It runs in families.

2. It is marked by high levels of circulating masculinizing hormones, leading to acne, hairiness, and weight gain, which suggests our masculine aspect, has been activated to defend us.

3. It's often linked to insulin resistance, similar to type 2 diabetes.

4. The surface of the ovary is covered by a white sheen beneath which are the ghosts of immature eggs that failed to develop sufficiently to be released at ovulation.

If women are programmed to develop and release an egg every month after puberty, what could have happened to disrupt this process? ***Since our ovaries and eggs represent not only our creativity but also our femininity, here are some extra questions to ask yourself if you've been diagnosed with PCOS:***

5. *If my eggs are failing to mature, was my own transition from girl to woman also stunted? Am I scared of becoming a woman?*

6. *Did I ever witness or experience deep wounding of the feminine, especially around puberty, whether through sexual abuse, betrayal, or abandonment, which caused my inner feminine to feel vulnerable and my inner masculine to rise up to protect me?*

7. *Do I find myself fighting to defend or justify myself?*

8. *Since insulin resistance suggests that we have difficulty accepting the sweetness of life, do I believe I'm lovable and deserve joy or do I push love away?*

If these questions stirred up any emotions or memories, I strongly advise you to seek professional help to heal the wounds of your own inner little girl and to relieve your inner masculine, who is probably exhausted trying to protect you. Remember, you're surrounded by the Great Mother's love, encouraging you to step forward as the beautiful and confident woman you were born to be.

CHAPTER 18

Our Womb; Our Sacred Temple

For centuries, the uterus has been deemed only to be important if you wanted to get pregnant, a myth perpetrated by the patriarchy some 3,000 years ago to persuade women to deny all of their unique gifts. But your womb or uterus is your powerhouse where all the magical transformation takes place.

Located within the protective pelvis, it's linked to the energy center known as the *sacral chakra or hara*, situated three fingers breadth below your navel. If you have experienced a hysterectomy or removal of your womb due to the presence of fibroids or any other gynecological problem, the womb's energetic form is always present, acting as a sacred chalice of wisdom, strength, and creativity.

In its non-pregnant state, the uterus is about the size of a small orange, yet few other organs of the body can match its transformative skills. During pregnancy, the ability to increase its size at full-term to that of a watermelon, and then to have the muscular strength to push the baby into the world, is amazing. In addition, it is also capable of not only changing a few cells into a beautiful baby but also taking old emotions and beliefs and turning them into blood to be shed during the menstrual period.

Our sacral chakra is also the energy center associated with all *relationships*, including our intimate ones. We're social beings and relationships are the cauldron in which we transform as souls; the more intense the emotions, the greater the growth. If you look at the list of emotions you have decided to release at the end of the month, you'll probably see that most come from our interactions with other people.

Viewed in this light, *our womb is a sacred temple*, where alchemy takes place, transforming simple substances into pure gold. It's time to honor our temple and ourselves as its high priestess, employing reliable doorkeepers to guard our precious womb!

Calling in Our Doorkeepers

I'd love to see every young girl being taught from an early age that her body, heart and especially her womb are priceless gifts from the Great Mother, which should be cared for in the same way that she cares for her most valued possessions. Hopefully, as she grows, she'll be surrounded by women who model respect for their bodies so that when this young priestess reaches puberty she'll delight in taking ownership of her precious sacred temple.

Let's take a walk through our sacred temple—the uterus—to get a sense of its general design. As with many spiritual buildings, the temple has an *outer door*—the vulva—that leads to a corridor—the vagina— at the end of which is the *inner door*—the cervix—that opens into the *inner sanctum*, our womb.

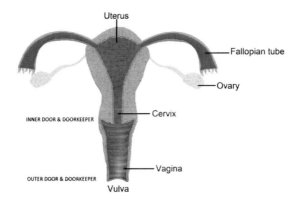

The uterus with its doorkeepers *(Artist Eran Cantrell)*

To protect and honor this temple, there are *guardians or doorkeepers* at each of the doors. The outer guardian can be described as the person who stands outside a building at the street level and advises you to remove your coat, switch off your cell phone, and lower your voice before stepping inside; like a bouncer!

The inner doorkeeper knows the importance of the inner sanctum and therefore only allows someone to enter if they meet certain criteria, which include honoring the sacred space and respecting the high priestess. The corridor between the doors helps us let go of unnecessary thoughts connected to the outer world and quiet our mind in preparation for entering a place of mystery and wonder.

I suggest you find time to meditate on your sacred temple and allow your intuition to guide you by revealing to you your outer and inner guardian. You may sense the doorkeepers as human, angelic, animal, or anything else; trust your intuition. You may also find that you're missing one or both doorkeepers, or that the doorkeepers are ineffectual at their job. You can provide mew instructions or even change your doorkeepers. If you're doing this exercise with young girls, you may call the outer door *the door of the body* and the inner door that of *the heart.*

Write your experiences of meeting your doorkeepers here:

I wonder how many of you find you have no doorkeepers or that the ones you did have were not serving your needs? The outer doorkeeper is usually a little more muscular than his fellow inner guardian who may take on a more ethereal role. My outer doorkeeper is a female hippopotamus with luscious long eyelashes! I've heard of guards who have fallen asleep on the job or have been too ineffectual to be taken seriously. At the other end of the scale, some women have reported that their doorkeepers scare everybody away; they've usually been hired to protect us after a past hurt or abuse.

Our doorkeepers are there to enrich self-respect and self-nurturing in all relationships. Although it's important to feel safe, we need to trust that there are people who will care for us in a loving way and let them enter into our sacred space, while refusing entrance to those who abuse us, whether sexually, physically or emotionally. With our guardians in place, we can move forward, although I suggest you check in with them once in a while to make sure they're still serving your needs effectively and unconditionally.

CHAPTER 19

Creating Healthy Boundaries

Do you ever feel overwhelmed by your family's emotions or find your-self trying to wriggle out of a dinner date with a friend as she always seems to drain your energy? Do you meet people and immediately want to change them because you think you know what's best for them? Do you ever feel your energy is being "*vampired*" but are unsure how to stop this?

It's natural for women to want to marinate everybody with love and juicy dragon energy in the hope that they will connect to their oneness. But it's also important to have healthy boundaries, respect our unique gifts, and accept that many people are very happy being miserable!

Taking on Emotions

I just want them to be happy, we tell ourselves, unconsciously pull-ing their undesirable emotions into our solar plexus, like a vacuum cleaner with a faulty filter, sending the energy down to the womb or sacral chakra to be stored and processed later. Maybe we tell ourselves that such empathy or emotional sensitivity is a sign of a caring nature when in truth, it may actually suggest that we have inadequate emo-tional boundaries and a palpable need to be needed. If you've ever said: *I'm sick to death of listening to that story again, I can't stomach it any-more,* it's your solar plexus screaming: *Help me, I'm overwhelmed with the problems and emotions of other people and I don't know how to say no!*

So much of our energy vacuuming occurs on an unconscious level; just by admitting we're an emotional sponge is the first step in making constructive changes. Only by acknowledging that we take on other people's feelings can we begin to clear out the stale energies that are often stored in our womb for years and start to see that many of the emotions we feel today don't even belong to us! Learning how to respect ourselves and clear our energy regularly is vitally important to our own health and happiness.

Here Are Some Suggestions to Create Healthy Boundaries & Maintain Optimal Energy Levels

1. If you feel stressed and tired, **surround yourself in a colored energy bubble,** choosing a color that feels right for you in the moment.

2. If someone's energy feels toxic, **imagine a mirror in front of you** with the reflective surface facing the other person so their emotions return to them.

3. Remember you **can't make someone happy or unhappy.**

4. Become a little more **selfish or self-full,** honoring your own needs.

5. Each evening, practice the ritual of **emptying your womb or 'bowl'** described below:

Emptying the Bowl

This practice is best done just before you go to bed as it will allow you a more restful sleep and to feel refreshed in the morning.

- *Find somewhere comfortable to lie or to sit and close your eyes.*

- *Using your breath let the out-breath be longer than the in-breath as you relax into your body.*

- *Allow your out-breath to gather up all the thoughts, feelings and energies you've picked up during the day and pour them into* your womb. If you no longer have a womb, you still have an energetic womb.

- Now through your womb see yourself standing on a shoreline at sunset. You can feel the ground under your feet, maybe sand or rock.

- Imagine you could take your womb out of your body and it becomes the most beautiful bowl.

- The bowl is full of old energy which you no longer wish to carry, some of it yours and some of the energy belongs to other people you've met during the day.

- When you are ready walk down to the water's edge and pour all the contents of the bowl into the water, knowing that water is the healing power of women

- Ask the Great Mother Water to take and transform this energy, washing away anything which separates you from the beautiful inner light at the base of the bowl.

- Kneel down and wash the bowl out, making sure nothing is stuck to its inner surface.

- Now you can see the beautiful light of your soul at the base of the bowl and you reconnect to who you are.

- As you walk back up the shore, you place the bowl back into your body cleaned and cleared.

- As you stand on the shore you can send your roots into Mother Earth and draw revitalizing, creative dragon energy up along the roots, your legs and then into your womb, ready for a good night's sleep and to feel refreshed at the start of another wonderful day.

Here's some sacred space to write your feelings and experiences of Emptying Your Bowl

Trying to Change Others

You may be thinking *I never do that,* but how often do you feel the need to offer an opinion, send someone an e-mail about the latest therapy, or become disappointed when a loved one refuses to listen to you? As women, we're can be obsessed with fixing or changing people, often under the disguise of caring: *It's only because I love you that I want you to change.* Just because you can intuitively see someone's potential, however, doesn't mean they want to change.

We energetically invite other people into our womb so we can marinate them in transformative dragon energy and there they sit, waiting for us to make it happen! Every time you're on the point of asking them to leave the womb (and perhaps even your life) as there appears to be no change in them, they come up with another excuse or plea to stay. But we're not helping ourselves or others by allowing them to take up residence in the womb. It's important to have the courage to say: ***I love you but it seems you're not ready to change. Please leave my sacred temple knowing it's available to you should you ever change your mind.***

Learning to know when to help and when to step back is vitally important for all relationships. And sometimes this involves accepting that the person who really needs to change—is us.

Dealing with Vampires

Our womb, with its juicy dragon energy, is like a honeypot containing the nectar of immortality that can transform a person's life if they can just reach our sacred temple. There are some people, men and women, who, unwilling to do their own inner work, prefer to steal this nectar, especially from someone who has poor doorkeepers or little interest in their sacred temple. This is one of the motives behind sexual abuse, although energetic sexual abuse or vampiring happens more often than you may think.

The entry point for the vampire is via the outer door or vulva that, linked to the base chakra, is particularly susceptible to fear-based threats or inappropriate sexual advances. You may actually feel sexually aroused as the vampire attempts to persuade you to let them enter your sacred temple through their seductive charms: *I feel so good around your energy, I feel so much better when we're together.* Watch out, they probably just want to access your honeypot!

Now before you see everybody as a vampire, there is one way to detect them. It may sound a little strange, but please do give it a try. If someone has entered your womb without permission, then when you think of a particular person, it will appear as if their feet are dangling out of your vagina! If you see or feel that this is true, imagine getting hold of their feet and pulling them out saying: **Get out NOW!** No niceties! Kick them out and shut the door.

As women, we're here to teach others to tap into their own creative power through their roots rather than trying to steal from *our* honeypot. We're only too happy to help them find their own power but they must ask with respect, honor, and humility, for we are high priestesses who love and respect ourselves first.

Spend some time reflecting on:

a. *Who have I been trying to help or change but now needs to ask to leave my sacred temple?*

b. *What relationship have I been trying to revive but which is truly over and I need to ask the person to leave?*

c. *Who presently, or in the past, has been vampiring my energy?*

d. *Where am I hanging onto someone even though my heart knows they do not nurture my soul, bring me pleasure or respect my needs?*

Disharmony of the Uterus: Fibroids

It's not uncommon for a woman in her menstrual years to have one or more fibroids. The first question I always ask is: *Who takes care of you?* At this point, she often bursts into tears and, with a definite note of resentment, answers: *I'm there for everybody else but nobody is there for me.* This response is partially true because it's probably more accurate for her to say: *I prefer to give to others as I'm actually terrified of receiving.* Here are some common beliefs that women may have, which make it difficult for us to receive:

- *Only weak people ask for help.*

- *I pride myself on being independent.*

- *I don't want to be vulnerable.*

- *What if I ask for something and they say No?*

- *What if what they offer is not what I want?*

- *What if there's a debt to pay after I accept their help, which they hold over me for years?*

Fibroids are often accompanied by heavy bleeding, suggesting a woman who is taking on the sadness of the world and crying for humanity.

Here are some recommendations if you have fibroids, to be used alongside any other therapy:

1. **Clear your womb** of all of those people who are perfectly capable of taking care of themselves, making space and time for you to relax and enjoy life.

2. Let family and friends know what they can do to **nurture your needs**.

3. **Be honest with your feelings**. If you feel irritated or resentful, journal about it or speak your feelings out loud and then say: *I need to make changes in my life, starting today!*

You'll be amazed how many people love you and want to nurture you if you just give them half a chance, and then you can send your Superwoman on a long overdue holiday!

CHAPTER 20

The Womb's Voice

Have you ever noticed that when a woman becomes tense or insecure, her speech becomes faster, higher, and louder? This is because when stressed, we speak from our throat and not our womb. As someone wise once remarked, the word *uterus* could also be described as our *utterer*; the place from which women *should* speak. But the womb is also the place where we store past emotions, especially from difficult relation-ships, which should have been released as blood during our period. But because we were probably unaware that our period provided this ser-vice, our womb is often full of old festering emotions that can be trig-gered when we're stressed.

So if we're in a situation which brings up memories of a previous dysfunctional relationship, we instinctively move our awareness from the sacral to the throat chakra, unwilling to disturb the painful emotions that have been carefully locked away in our uterus. The only problem is that since our power is seated in our uterus, when we speak from the throat we often feel that our personal needs and opinions go unheard.

If you want to see the effect of this shift, listen to a woman speak-ing from her throat; it's often hard to engage with the conversation as their voice is a monotone that lacks emotionality and her subject matter is full of information and details. I often feel that she's trying to convince me of something she intellectually wants to believe, but the truth is still buried, as her heart and womb are not engaged.

When she moves her awareness into her womb, however, you'll notice an immediate shift as she connects to a deeper and more authentic truth. The words are more heartfelt, the pace slower, and her voice becomes full of rhythm and interesting emotion, all of which encourage you to engage. This makes good sense, given that the sacral chakra is the center of relationship.

So if you want to be heard, breathe out deeply, sending your roots into Mother Earth. Then draw the dragon energy into your womb and speak without apology and with deep respect for who you are as a woman, bursting with wisdom and power. You'll find that you take more time to consider your words as you can feel them emerging from a deep knowing rather than just satisfying a need to provide information. It's also interesting to see that when you root your energy in this way, any woman you're talking to will, subconsciously shift her energy into her womb, making conversations far more harmonious.

Finding the Right Answer

I don't know about you, but sometimes when I'm asked to make a decision, my mind goes crazy trying to make the right choice that will satisfy everybody. It's overloaded and busy, assessing all the emotions and expectations involved. Sadly, when I do this I often find that, in my desire to please everyone else, I've forgotten to consider my own needs.

Here's a simple intuitive exercise to help you find an answer that nurtures your needs. When you do this, I can assure you that your relationships will become much more satisfying for all concerned.
Sit quietly and close your eyes. Bring into your awareness a question pertaining to a decision you have to make such as whether or not to visit an acquaintance. Take the question first to your head; listen to the answer. Then take the same question to your heart and listen to the answer.

Finally, take the question to your womb and the indwelling dragon; hear the answer.

Write your answers

Did you notice any difference between the answers?

I commonly find that my head will tell me the logical thing to do with lots of "shoulds and musts." My heart on the other hand, with a huge amount of help from my solar plexus, often reminds me of the emotional impact of my decision on the happiness of other people.

But when I listen to my womb, the answer is clear and crone-like, caring only for my inner well-being. Not wasting words, I'll perhaps hear: *Of course you're not going to visit, you don't like her!*

Listening to our womb is the only way to be honest, non-manipulative, and clear in our decisions, making life so much easier!

Respect

The one quality that every living being on this planet deserves is respect. I often say: Y*ou don't need to like me, understand me or even love me, but please respect me.* Mild disrespect includes when someone pretends to listen but their attention is elsewhere or when we're spoken to in a patronizing or demeaning manner. In more extreme cases, disrespect turns into obvious abuse, which can be emotional, physical, or sexual.

I'm particularly affected when women don't respect each other for we have a natural desire to bond. Whenever I feel unheard or unseen by a woman, I will stop speaking, check that my roots are deeply in Mother Earth and that my womb is full of dragon energy, and then say clearly: **Please respect me.** You'll be amazed how your interactions will change when you speak from your womb, for what you're saying is: *I respect myself and I want to respect you. Let's work at this together.*

CHAPTER 21

Sexuality and Sensuality

We now arrive at a topic that, with so much public exposure, would seem to have little mystery still to share: *sex*. But don't be fooled. You may think you learned all you needed to know about sex as a teenager, but there's so much more to this sacred art, taking lovemaking to a whole new level of enjoyment and satisfaction.

This simple three-letter word carries with it such a wide range of experiences, emotions, and expectations, ranging from romance and intimacy through to pornography and even rape. In a relationship, it can certainly feed our needs and desires but how can we make sure it feeds our heart and soul?

Let's look at why sex is so important to us and the role our dragon energy plays in it. On an esoteric level, there are just two processes: *birth, the creation of duality from the state of oneness, and sex: the unification of two different forces usually culminating in orgasmic bliss.*

Because women always seek to unite and connect, we are in essence sexual beings, providing the means by which we, and any partner, can achieve unification or wholeness via our serpentine ladder. Nobody makes us sexual or sensual; we are naturally sensual and we create our sexuality; it's time to own these strengths without shame or apology. No woman is asexual; the question is whether we trust and love ourselves enough to develop and enjoy our serpentine ladder, prohibiting anybody to enter it without our full permission.

Sexual priestesses, in days gone by, would wear rings or bracelets in the shape of serpents or snakes to denote that they were a *hierodulai,* or "sacred woman" trained in the ways of transformation through mastery of their sexual dragon energy. This term was later translated into English as *harlot* and into German as *hore,* which became the English *whore.* But at no point was the name meant to be derogatory, for it literally means "beloved one."

The serpentine ladder is magnetic in quality; attracting or drawing into itself. So when we have sex with another person, we're energetically drawing them into our base chakra while, at the same time, encompassing them in their new creative potential. Together, we then travel up along our ladder until we reach the crown chakra, where this potential is ignited bringing realization of their true self, at orgasm. During the journey from base to crown chakra, awareness or consciousness changes from instinctual to magnificent; alchemical transformation.

I wonder how many of you know that when you enter into lovemaking with a male partner, you're offering him an incredibly profound experience, for it's much more difficult for him to reach such giddy heights without a woman. We women can, however, readily travel along our ladder without a partner during our periods, in labor, after menopause, or during masturbation.

Time to reflect on your own sexual experiences:

1. *What 3 words or adjectives encompass my feelings about sex or making love today?*

2. *What turns me on? What are my most erogenous zones?*

3. *When was my first sexual experience? How would I describe that experience?*

4. *What was I told as a young girl about sex, masturbation, flirting & sensuality?*

5. *Would I describe my mother as a sexual being?*

6. *Have I been sexually abused or raped? What scars has this left?*

7. *Presently, how often do I make love (with a partner)?*

8. *Do I pleasure myself (masturbate) when alone or with a partner?*

9. *What changes would I like to make in my future sex life?*

* * *

I'd like you to imagine that you're a young girl preparing for womanhood and you've been invited to join a circle of wise women at 3:00 a.m. to hear their wisdom. Worried that the whole subject of sacred sexuality may be too serious, you're delighted to hear the laughter ring out as the women share their experiences, although it's clear that they treat the subject with great reverence. Now sit back and listen as each woman takes a turn sharing her wisdom:

1. **Sensuality and sexuality are not the same**. Enjoying your body's sensuality enhances mental and physical wellbeing

Wisdom: *Even babies within the womb have been seen to enjoy the sensual pleasure of touching their bodies. Just massaging yourself with body lotions is a lovely way to get to know the different sensations of your gorgeous body.*

2. With your doorkeepers and womb guardian in place, **anybody who enters your body should respect and honor who you** are as a high priestess and the enormous gift you're offering them through the act of sexual intercourse. Sexual abuse is an immoral attempt to gain access to the dragon power stored in the womb and serpentine ladder. However, without gaining permission, they cannot ascend the ladder.

Wisdom: *Don't allow anybody into your body unless they respect and honor you and your beautiful body.*

3. As humans, sex is less about impregnation and more about **making love** with the most powerful effect being achieved when we face our partner, heart to heart.

Wisdom: *Respect, trust and magic occur when hearts touch.*

4. Just giving **oral sex can be a one-sided affair**.

Wisdom: *Sex should be equally enjoyable and gratifying for both parties.*

5. Once you **share your juices** with another person (either by vaginal or oral sex) you create an emotional and energetic bond with that person for the next three years.

Wisdom: *Given that this bond is formed, you may wish to think before you have sex with someone who you don't know very well or don't particularly like.*

6. **The stronger your magnetic field,** the greater the experience for all concerned.

It's therefore imperative that your partner lay aside their personal needs to attend to *what turns you on*—romance, touch, and words—and which particular erogenous zones need to be stimulated to *light up* your magnetic field. Without your arousal and the activation of the serpentine ladder, intercourse is essentially ineffective for all concerned, with awareness remaining at the base chakra level.

Wisdom: *If you're not sexually aroused and energetically lit up, don't have sex.*

7. Sex at the base chakra level meets an instinctual need to release energy and experience a short-lived high. But if you want **sex and relationship**, then the process moves to the sacral chakra, and requires greater levels of intimacy and trust.

Wisdom: *Communicate clearly whether you just want sex or sex and relationship, otherwise you can be left feeling abused and disappointed.*

8. Intimacy at the sacral chakra with another person transitions into intimacy with our deepest self or soul at the heart chakra, turning **love making** with another person into love making with ourselves.

Wisdom: *If it's difficult for us to truly love ourselves and to surrender to such love, any orgasm remains as a purely energetic affair.*

9. A woman's most **sexually sensitive organ is her clitoris**, its tiny head covered with sexually charged nerve endings. Believe it or not, it's actually approximately eight inches in length; so if size matters, women win!

Wisdom: *Enjoy the power of your clitoris; it's your most erogenous zone.*

10. **Twenty-five percent of women never experience an orgasm** and of those who do, only fifteen to twenty percent experience this through vaginal penetration alone. Yet seventy-five percent of men continue to offer only penetrative sex to their female partners. Apart from the small proportion of women who possess a G-spot on their anterior vaginal wall, there is very little sensual tissue in the vagina or cervix, otherwise we'd all orgasm during our Pap or cervical smears procedures! Most women require at least clitoral stimulation alongside vaginal stimulation to experience an orgasm.

Wisdom: *Trust the feelings of your own body, not what someone, even your boyfriend, tells you to feel.*

11. **Sixty-seven percent of women fake orgasms.** The problem is that if you fake orgasms, there's a good chance you'll lie about other things in your relationship. Sadly, many men still focus on their needs which may be satisfied in a few minutes, rather than realizing that they can experience greater pleasure by focusing on the longer period of foreplay to light up their partner's magnetic field.

Wisdom: *There is nothing wrong with you; you were born to be a beautiful, sensual woman who deserves to be highly honored and pleasured.*

12. Orgasm is much easier when you can **relax and trust your partner.** If you don't orgasm, don't feel shame but rather see that your body is protecting you; find help to understand the deeper

messages. Self-pleasure is a wonderful way of trusting your body to guide you toward orgasm.

Wisdom: *Masturbation is a healthy activity for all women, whatever your age; it keeps the juices flowing.*

13. **Sex is one of the most intimate experiences for a man.** For a man to enter a woman, he must agree to surrender his control or ego needs if he wants his energy to progress into the sacral chakra. Esoterically, he needs to agree to leave his armor, sword, and masks at the outer door —the vulva—so he can approach the womb with soft humility. When a man refuses sex or only has it with strangers, he's often fearful of losing control and being embraced by love.

Wisdom: *Intimacy, trust, and surrender are essential for a sexual relationship.*

14. Thus, once a man enters a woman, **he needs to surrender control of the process**, allowing the woman to manage the rhythm using her powerful vaginal muscles. Unfortunately, it's far more common for a man to set the rhythm through his thrusts.

Wisdom: *Time for change, ladies! By practicing rhythmically tightening and relaxing the vaginal muscles, you'll be ready to take the lead and your sexual experiences will go to a whole new level for both of you.*

15. Taking time to **travel up the serpentine ladder together** is an exquisite experience, especially as you pass through the heart chakra and you fall into timeless love.

Wisdom: *The journey is as important as the goal; enjoy.*

16. The final stage of love making occurs when we release our hold on an individual identity and **surrender to our spiritual self at the crown chakra**. Now at the peak of the experience, the dragon

energy stimulates the release of the mind-altering hormone DMT from the pineal gland and we explode into multidimensional awareness: ecstatic bliss.

Wisdom: *It's fabulous to be able to bathe in this spiritual energy whether on our own or with another person, experiencing healing, peace, and relaxation.*

Sex is not only a physical event between two people; it is an amazing expression of love. It's time to lift this sacred act from the dark place of secrets, seduction, and shame, into the light, where its intimacy, enjoyment, and spiritual evolution are celebrated.

CHAPTER 22

Pregnancy and Birth

For most mothers, giving birth and watching one's children grow is one of the most satisfying and profound aspects of being a woman. Like all things that are feminine, pregnancy has three phases or trimesters, which are quite distinct.

The First Trimester

As the newly pregnant mother adjusts to the flush of hormones and the change in status, it's a good time to self-nurture by getting plenty of rest and eating healthy food. This helps the developing baby who is going through its own amazing process, transforming from a few cells into a tiny but almost fully formed human being by the end of thirteen weeks. There are so many little details to get right for both the fetus and placenta that it's not surprising most miscarriages occur during this time. On average, 15 percent of pregnancies end in miscarriage before the twentieth week, with 80 percent of those occurring in the first trimester, maybe even before the woman even knew she was pregnant.

When I worked in obstetrics, early miscarriages were often viewed as Mother Nature's way of taking care of the fetus by giving it the best possible start in life. This may be a rather innocent approach, but it concerns me that today, with so many modern tests and the ability to plan a pregnancy with such precision, these early miscarriages so commonly lead to feelings of failure. There are many reasons why a pregnancy doesn't go beyond thirteen weeks. Hopefully, I can reassure you that if a soul is meant to be part of your life, it is extremely patient and will wait around for the perfect conditions!

The Second Trimester

With high levels of progesterone—*the relaxing hormone*—and prolactin—*the nesting hormone*—the next thirteen weeks are usually much more settled, with the mother feeling more content and energetic. At around twenty weeks the baby's first movements are usually felt—*the quickening*. Esoterically this fluttering is caused by the initial passage of the soul into the developing human body, although the soul doesn't tend to fully inhabit the body until just before birth.

The Third Trimester

After a relatively calm few months, the last trimester heralds the end of the pregnancy and the beginning of a new and unique life. Although there is often more physical discomfort, many women continue working right up to a few weeks before their due date.

Labor

Our ancient sisters would never have allowed men into the birthing chamber! They believed that only women, including female midwives, doulas, mothers, and sisters, should attend women's matters. Although I love watching a father tend for his wife and then marvel at the sight of his gorgeous new baby, I believe women should always be in control of the birth process, while men can help! I welcome the return of home deliveries, where birth can be seen as less of a clinical issue and more of a natural process.

I want to mention an extraordinary meeting between the soul of the mother and that of the child just prior to birth. If, as a woman in labor, you're able to synchronize your breathing with the waves of contractions, you'll find yourself being carried up your own serpentine path toward your crown chakra. As the pineal gland is stimulated by the contractions, you'll notice your awareness has changed

and you'll be able to recognize and embrace the soul of your baby, fulfilling the contract you made to each other before either of you was born. Then, as the desire to push increases, your focus will once again descend to the sacral chakra, bringing the beloved soul of your baby with you, to be anchored by you into its physical body. Then, with an ecstatic and orgasmic cry that resonates with the sound all women have made from the beginning of time, your child is born and all is well.

Cesarean Section (C-section)

I can't leave this discussion without mentioning the rise in the number of Cesarean sections being performed today; presently 35 percent in the United States and in some countries, as high as 80%. Whereas this emergency operation can be lifesaving for mother and child, when a labor runs into difficulties, elective C-sections should be reserved for births where vaginal delivery would be impossible or dangerous. Unfortunately, C-sections are now also being used as a convenience so that the busy schedules of both doctors and mothers can be accommodated, or because a C-section operation is more financially advantageous for the hospital.

Birth is not a medical problem but a natural process embracing some of the greatest mysteries of womanhood. Modern healthcare offers many benefits to mother and child, who in previous times, may otherwise have died in childbirth. Be this as it may, there is still so much we don't understand about the process and how our interference may impact the future well-being of both mother and child.

If you have given birth, what were some of the most magical moments and were some of the challenges?

CHAPTER 23

Breast Care

Did you know we're the only mammals who have fully developed breasts from puberty onward, even when we're not pregnant, and that unlike other animals, our breasts are not safely hidden, but proudly surround our heart chakra for all to see? Clearly our breasts serve additional purposes beyond the provision of nourishment for an infant. Their position and softness suggest that they also offer comfort and safety, which is very evident when a baby lingers after a feed, or your child reaches out for a hug. I believe the breasts, situated on either side of the *heart chakra*, help to enhance its energy, so that a woman's love radiates out toward everyone she meets. Though I do need to say, larger breasts do not necessarily correlate to greater love!

When a baby suckles at the breast, the hormone oxytocin is released into the bloodstream of both mother and child. Known as the *"love hormone,"* oxytocin stimulates the desire for intimate bonding—leading to trust, calmness, and security for both individuals. Research shows that our blood levels of oxytocin in our first six months of life greatly influence our ability to create meaningful and close relationships later in life and that our early levels of oxytocin are increased when there is eye to eye contact with our mother, tender touch, and when she speaks to us with a loving voice. Studies also show that if our mother received little intimate nurturing when she was a child, not only will her oxytocin levels be deficient but there's a good chance that she'll have difficulty bonding with us and she may be experiencing *social isolation as an adult.*

For a woman, such isolation can have deep effects, not only on her psyche but also on her body, given that women find strength, security, and well-being through connection with other women. It's now known that young women who feel lonely and alienated are more likely to experience peri-menopausal symptoms, osteoporosis, and heart disease later on. This is why it's so important for us to develop close circles of girlfriends throughout our life where trust, honesty, respect, and compassion are the keywords, giving us the freedom to share our innermost joys and fears without judgment.

Our Breasts and the First Five Years of a Child's Life

For nine months the baby floats in the sacred waters of its mother's womb, still attached spiritually to the Great Mother's loving energy. Leaving this relatively quiet and peaceful state is quite a shock to the baby's system, which is why it's so important to lay the baby on its mother's heart chakra as soon as possible after birth, so it can be comforted by love.

Human mothers are the intermediary between the spiritual mother and Mother Earth, the latter eventually becoming the source of nourishment, security, and creativity for the growing child and adult. In many indigenous cultures, children are raised amongst women for their first five years of life in order to develop self-confidence, security, and allow for social bonding.

Over time, they're weaned from the mother onto Mother Earth so that by the age of five they're ready to start school and mix with their peers and other adults. This is done with the reassurance that they can always return to their mother's embrace when in need of comfort.

But these transitions from spiritual mother to birth mother to Earth Mother are not always smooth and are often the source of pain and anxiety, possibly contributing to issues of both the heart and breast at a later date.

Too *Little* Love

Whether a mother chooses to breastfeed or not, holding her baby to the breast is a magical experience, marinating both mother and child in self-confidence and love. If for whatever reason, a girl is pushed off the breast/heart chakra too early, she may be forced to grow up too quickly. Having perceived that her first role model, her mother, has rejected her, she may become overly independent and experience difficulty trusting others, especially other women. She may also have a poor relationship with spiritual love, perceiving that she was also abandoned by her spiritual mother. It's common for such women to prefer to listen to their intellect rather than their feminine intuition, and to develop masculine attributes while shunning their feminine self, as it appears to carry the pain of vulnerability and rejection.

There are many reasons why a mother can't offer breastmilk, including the fact that she may not have received adequate nurturing herself during childhood. A mother busy with work and taking care of others may appear not to care. Just making special time for cuddles is important for all children, especially before the age of five. Healing wounds of separation and the belief that we're unlovable is so important, especially when our fiercely independent persona with its impenetrable barriers is excluding the very love we seek. When you have the courage to start to demolish your own walls and ask for help, you'll be amazed how much love will pour in.

Too *Much* Love

It may surprise you that a child can be held too long on the breast, which may also lead to problems. Smothering love is often a sign of a mother's need for solace and companionship due to her own loneliness or insecurity in adult relationships.

By the time the child reaches five, there may even have been a role reversal wherein the daughter mothers the parent. In this, she has become emotionally responsible for her mother's well-being, and is unable to leave "home" in case something happens to her mother. Because the mother is dependent on the child, she will purposely fail to root her into the loving embrace of Mother Earth, causing the daughter to lack self-identity, personal boundaries, and the confidence to leave home and walk away. Without the connection to Mother Earth, there is usually an over-identification with the spirit world, where life seems easier.

Having the courage to build healthy personal boundaries and cut the emotional ties with our parents takes time and often the help of a good therapist and supportive women friends, all of whom provide a safe place to embrace one's own beautiful self.

Take time to reflect on breast nurturing, writing the thoughts below:

1. *Do I feel that my mother nurtured me and my needs when I was young?*

2. *Was I breast fed as a baby; if so for how long?*

3. *Do I believe I was pushed off the breast too early? What were the circumstances?*

4. *Do I believe I was held too long at the breast? Why was this?*

5. *Today, do I have any issues trusting women or letting them help me?*

Breast Cancer Care and Prevention

I've spent my working life as a doctor, looking at the possible messages behind disease, knowing that illness is not a sign of weakness or failure but a message from the loving soul that something has to change. These thoughts are complementary to any other treatments you may be taking and are available to all women as breast care.

When I developed breast cancer in 2011, my immediate thought was: *Wow, my soul really loves me as only this would have stopped me in my tracks!* I always knew that breast cancer was about self-love but my own cancer taught me so much more. If you mention self-love to most women, they'll tell you how they nurture themselves with regular massages and other forms of self-care. But in my case, I realized it was much more than that: I'd lost the self that needed to be loved.

My cancer taught me that I was, and still am, to a certain extent, a *pleaser*, keen to be of service to others even when they don't want my help! From an early age I believed that my life was much easier if I put aside my emotional needs to meet the needs of others, using my intuitive skills to read what they wanted before they asked. I was so focused on being responsible for others that I lost myself.

The suggestions below are for all women. I call it breast care because when we care for our breasts, we care for everything inside us which is soft, vulnerable, and lovable.

1. **Let go of the need to take care of everybody's feelings.** You can't make someone happy or unhappy.

2. **Surprise your family and friends by being more self-centered**, expressing feelings and asking for help, without the need to worry about the impact of your demands on their lives.

3. **Send your inner pleaser and *Miss Nice* on holiday and welcome** home your inner *Bitch*, which is probably in alliance with your inner dragon.

4. **Rather than saying "*Yes*" right away**, listen to your wise womb and ask: *What do I feel? What do I want?* Become self-full not self-less.

5. **Say "*No*" and mean it.** Leave out "*Maybe later*", or attempts to explain or justify your decision.

6. **It is okay to express your anger** as it gives you a chance to be clear about your feelings. Then move on.

7. **Remember, you're a beautiful high priestess** and let people serve you.

8. **Cut the emotional ties** with those people who make you feel small and don't respect you.

9. **If anything you're about to do starts with *should***, don't do it.

10. **Wear bras without wires** to ease the flow of energy around your breasts; there's little reason for wires and padding except for fashion.

CHAPTER 24

Menopause and Beyond: Entering Years of Wisdom and Power

Welcome to the menopause; a beautiful rite of passage moving us from our mothering years to years of deep wisdom and creativity as we embrace the role of crone or wise woman. Officially, menopause is defined as having taken place a year after our last period, with the average age for its onset being around fifty-one. But it's more accurate to look at the whole transition period—the *perimenopause*—which lasts between eight and twelve years, beginning in our mid to late forties and ending around fifty-four. These are years of preparation; letting go of old patterns and making way for a wiser and more content you. That's why it's often called "the change."

My advice to any woman in her mid-forties?
Bring balance and self-nurturing into your life today!

Menopause affects not only our body but also our psyche, moving our focus away from seeking personal success to a more collective vision where we can use our gifts and talents to ensure an abundant and healthy future for the next seven generations of children. It often coincides with our children leaving home, when we can dedicate more time to nurturing our deeper dreams and less to nurturing others. This can be a challenge for those women who start their families in their forties, given that they may find their mothering instincts clashing with the desires of the incoming crone who demands more personal time.

Three Stages of Womanhood

A woman passes through three major stages of womanhood during her life. In the first stage, we're the *maiden or virgin* holding our seeds of creative potential in our ovaries, awaiting puberty. The second stage covers our *menstrual or mothering years* when we can give birth every month not only to babies but also to new ideas. These monthly cycles hopefully teach us how to balance the three phases of the creative cycle: *growth, nurturing, and release.* If we don't achieve this balance, we'll probably be amongst the 60 percent of women who suffer from PMS and menstrual issues.

The process of building a self-assured identity reaches its peak in our *mid to late forties* when ideally we will have a healthy ego, know how to relax and self-nurture, and be happy to die to old energies and reconnect to the Great Mother's creative juices every month. If this is true, then it's easier for us to transition from *mothering to crone or wise-woman* energy, ready to enjoy our postmenopausal years full of pleasure, fulfillment, and contentment. If all these requirements have not been met, then our perimenopausal years provide us with plenty of opportunities to uncover the self that has been buried for years in busyness, complacency, appeasement, or in taking care of others.

Perimenopause: Years of Change and Challenge

Maybe you'll sail through the change, saying: What menopause?

However, 70 percent of women experience a bumpy perimenopause, with symptoms that include hot flashes (flushes), insomnia, anxiety, headache, fatigue, bowel and urinary disturbances, depression, and a fuzzy mind. Eighty percent of women with PMS go on to experience menopausal symptoms.

Rise of the Dark Goddess

I believe it's important to understand that many of the issues of menopause arise because we're being forced to embrace the full strength of the crone—the dark goddess—for her time has come! Of the three aspects of womanhood, the dragon energy is most potent when held in her hands, making post- menopause our most effective years as women. This is because the power is no longer merely invested in personal desires but is available for dreams that will change consciousness—nothing can stop us now!

I'd also like to add that the absence of menopausal symptoms does not necessarily mean that you've embraced your dragon energy. It may still be languishing beneath your feet, waiting for you to make space in your womb and your life for its appearance. Maybe it's time to take the risk, it's worth it!

I've met a number of women who, unwilling to be called a crone, attempt to prolong the mother phase by adding a fourth aspect of the goddess: the matriarch. I'm sorry, four is not a female number and perhaps all we're trying to do is hope that we never have to meet our dark goddess! Archetypically, this face of the feminine is very comfortable embracing all aspects of dragon power, including those that are destructive, seductive, and manipulative. When I suggest that these properties exist within every woman, I'm often met with astonishment and denial. But until we accept and master all the faces of dragon energy, we'll never be truly in our power.

The Greatest Challenge to the Empowerment of Women Is Fear of Our Dark Power

Before you run away screaming, let me reassure you that once you meet and accept this part of yourself, you don't need to live with it every day. It can hang in your closet as a piece of clothing that you can choose to wear but no longer fear.

Becoming Mistress of Our Dragon after Menopause

When our periods end, we lose the physical connection to Mother Earth and, if we're not adequately rooted into her soil, the unopposed creative dragon energy can now race upward through our body causing mayhem to our emotions and hormones, leading to irrational anxiety, hot flashes, headaches, and insomnia as we struggle to keep our feet on the ground. Finding ways to master—or mistress—our dragon energy during the perimenopausal years is vitally important because now there's no way of putting the dragon back in the box, for now it has only one boss, the crone or dark goddess!

CHAPTER 25

Taming the Menopausal Dragon

As we transition from mother to crone, we're being asked to face all the personal issues—often carried from childhood—that would prevent us from bringing detached compassion to the tasks that face us as a postmenopausal woman. If we're still trying to meet our ego needs after menopause, our effectiveness as a crone will be diminished.

To make sure we sail through our peri-menopause, it's good to look at these questions and address any issues as we approach our late forties. Even if you are post-menopausal it's really important to review these questions as it never too late to enrich your wise woman powers.

1. *Even though I pretend not to care, where do I lack self-confidence and still look for approval?*

2. *Am I ruled by my mind? Can I switch off my mind and relax?*

3. *Am I an expert at "reading" the energy of other people to stay safe?*

4. *Am I ready to listen to my needs for once?*

5. *Do I take on the worries and emotions of my family and even the world?*

6. *Have I experienced trauma in my life that causes me to be hypervigilant? Is it time to engage the help of a professional therapist to deal with this distress?*

7. *Can I step back and serve humanity at a more expansive level?*

8. *Where am I still acting from fear and not love?*

9. *Do I have a group of friends who know me at a deep and trusting level?*

10. *Can I let others into my life to take care of me?*

Hypersensitivity

As we pass through the perimenopause, we become more sensitive to psychic impressions and hence more intuitive and insightful. However, our expanded awareness is probably the reason why some postmenopausal women complain of claustrophobia, which had never been a problem in the past. We may also have difficulty listening to conversations in noisy places and find that certain aromas act as irritants, which never happened when we were young. By accepting that we are more sensitive and intuitive in our postmenopausal years, we can make choices which honor our gifts and avoid situations that aggravate our beautifully enriched nervous system.

Anxiety and Insomnia

Prior to menopause, the impact of stress in our lives is lessened by the protective qualities of estrogen and progesterone. But this benefit is lost when we enter the perimenopausal years, causing us to feel the full force of the stress hormones—adrenaline and cortisone—and to face emotions we've probably been trying to avoid for a long time. This can lead to increased levels of anxiety and insomnia.

If you have ever suffered from this, it feels as if you're going crazy, especially as the symptoms seem to come out of blue and have little relevance to your ordinary life. For instance, you may wake with feelings of dread, irrational anxiety, rapid heartbeat, and unexplained depression. Any additional stress can tip you over the edge, causing more physical symptoms such as diarrhea, headaches, and breathing difficulties. The anxiety can continue into the night, causing insomnia with frequent waking.

To understand the symptoms, here's a useful analogy: The train has come to a halt but the engine is still running at full speed, motivated by a deep-rooted belief that we have to keep going and cannot allow ourselves to relax. Perimenopause says: *It's time to not only stop the engine, but to step off the train and rest.*

Here's a simple exercise to quieten anxiety:
Breathing into Relaxation: Breathe in for the count of 3. Now breathe out fully, right down to your feet for the count of 6. Hold your breath out for as long as you can before taking the next in-breath, and repeat until you feel your mind and heart relaxing.

Hot Flushes/Flashes

Is it hot in here or is it just me? With these words we start stripping off clothes or kicking off the sheets, as surges of heat and dripping perspiration cause us to seek immediate relief. Around 70 percent of women experience hot flushes and/or night sweats during their menopausal years.

Hot flashes are often worse when we're anxious or stressed because, believe it or not, these soaking wet sweats are the body's way of calming us down. During episodes of stress, the sympathetic nervous system limits the flow of blood to unnecessary systems, including our skin, so it becomes dry and cool. Once the stress has passed, our parasympathetic system takes over and dissipates the heat that has built up in the body by causing us to sweat. Hot flashes are not the enemy but our friend, washing away anxiety and stress so that we can relax.

By facing our stressors and moving into relaxation naturally, the frequency and intensity of our hot flashes will lessen.

Here Are Some More Suggestions to Reduce Anxiety, Insomnia, and Hot Flashes

a. Take long **deep out-breaths** through the body, rooting yourself into Mother Earth.

b. **Avoid multitasking** as this keeps you in your head and doesn't allow relaxation.

c. Take up **creative activities** that offer both a community spirit and an outlet for dragon energy.

d. Make **quality time for girlfriends**; togetherness greatly reduces stress in women.

e. **Reduce stimulants** such as alcohol, caffeine, and smoking.

f. **Switch off the hypervigilant or overactive mind** by dancing, singing, and laughing.

g. **Let go of the need to be everything** to all people; release excess emotions into Mother Earth.

h. **Love your anger**; and if you feel angry, do something to change an unreasonable situation.

i. **Take warm baths** with lavender and Epsom salts to relax the body.

j. Meet and **embrace your dark goddess** and her faithful dragon.

Weight Changes

It's not uncommon for women to change shape and weight at menopause, with many of us thickening at the waist and becoming a little heavier on the bottom, resonating with the shape of Mother Earth! The transformation of my body meant clothes shopping went from being a pleasurable experience to a battle with the fashion industry, given that I refuse to accept that I can't look gorgeous and sexy after sixty!

Extra fat stores do actually provide us with an additional source of estrogen, which in turn can reduce menopausal symptoms, although excess gain can lead to other problems such as diabetes, heart disease, and arthritis. But I think there's another, more esoteric reason for the weight gain; it's the body's way of providing ballast to the rising dragon energy and when we learn to keep ourselves rooted and tame the beast, then we'll have less need for those extra pounds!

CHAPTER 26

Post-menopause: Freedom, Contentment, and Community

I read a lovely story about the power of Grandmothers to change the world just by standing silently together in a park. Many of the people who passed the group wondered what they were doing as they didn't seem to be protesting or have anything to sell. Someone even called the police, but since they were not disturbing the peace, there was no reason to move them on. Slowly more and more Grandmothers gathered. They stood proudly, without the need to express any particular emotion; their fearless and well-rooted presence was more powerful than any words [1].

This collective energy reminds me of the Clan Mothers whose wisdom and detachment from personal needs could selflessly decide what was best for their people. When enough postmenopausal women fully embody the clear sight and determination of the crone, I can envision a group of them standing outside buildings where abuse, greed, deception, and corruption are rampant, and quietly saying: *We see you, we know what you're doing, and we will remain here until you stop.*

Such Grandmother energy is not just related to age or whether or not you have grandchildren. Instead it depends on whether you have passed through the perimenopause, releasing your fears and emotional needs and are now ready to stand in your steady power, embodying the dreams and ideas that will create an abundant and peaceful world for the next seven generations.

* * *

Many women still enjoy work years after their menopause or have taken on a role that fully satisfies their needs. Others are treasuring their time with grandchildren, a very different experience from having one's own children. As you've heard throughout this handbook, we are just as creative and aligned to the lunar cycles after menopause as we were before. In fact, we're *more* powerful, for we now embody a sense of freedom that we may never have experienced before. With nothing to prove, we can choose to be with the people who nurture our soul, spend time in pastimes that feed our inner passions, and be honest with ourselves and others, saying "*No*" and meaning it!

If this doesn't sound like you, you may wish to reread the list of questions at the beginning of the last chapter. Did you skip the opportunities offered by perimenopause and are now struggling to release old emotional needs that hamper your ability to step fully into your Grandmother role?

I remember listening to an elegant group of women in their nineties, all of whom were just as vibrant and passionate as they had been half a century earlier. Each was asked in turn: **What is the secret of a good life as a crone?** Here are their answers:

- **Find a passion** and pursue it until it reaches its conclusion.

- **Follow the sun and the seasons** when planning your day; when we are in harmony with Mother Earth, life becomes sweeter.

- **Spend time with young people**, sharing your wisdom and letting their energy inspire you.

- **Keep your mind active** with news of events, both local and global.

- **Remember that age** is just a number.

We desperately need true Grandmother energy to take the lead on this planet at this time. Join me in an imaginary park and together let's build new levels of integrity, respect, and compassion for the women and children of today and for those who will walk upon our planet for the next one thousand years.

1. Sharon Mehdi: *The Great Silent Grandmother Gathering: a story for anybody who thinks she can't save the world.*

CHAPTER 27

Following Our Intuition

*Do you intuitively know it's time to make changes, but are
procrastinating because you're fearful of upsetting the status quo and
facing the unknown?*

*Have you ever failed to speak or act on an intuitive hunch and now live
with regret?*

If you answered yes to these questions, you're not alone. These are
typical responses to the voice of our soul, the intuition, whose messages
often appear out of the blue, making us question our current course of
action and long held beliefs. This loving inner voice arises out of the
energy between the heart chakra and third eye. It never abandons us,
always encouraging us not to be small but to have the courage to trust
the compassionate soul which offers a happier and more abundant life
on all levels.

In essence, following through on the messages of our feminine
intuition is the journey of embodying women's mysteries. By emptying our mind and womb and connecting to the wisdom of our inner
dragon and soul, we are inspired to manifest our true spiritual potential,
becoming eternally healed or whole.

Our capacity to hear our intuitive voice depends on our ability to let go of the masculine logical mind and become innocent or curious like a child.

**INNOCENCE = IN NO SENSE (Out of your mind) =
INNER SENSE (Intuition)**

Here are some simple exercises to clear the mind, connect to the soul, and receive inspiration, while at the same time allowing the body to release stress and become revitalized with precious energy.

A. **Using the Breath to Rebalance your Energies.**

This meditation can be used any time you feel overstretched or overwhelmed with thoughts and emotions and disconnected from your truth.

1. **Empty:** *On the next breath, breathe in for the count of 3 then out for the count of 6. Imagine your out-breath gathering all the stress from your mind, then from your body, and releasing it into Mother Earth. Repeat three times.*

2. **Connect:** *Now at the end of the next cycle focus on the ground beneath your feet, hold your breath out for a count of between 4 and 6 and connect to your deep knowing. Repeat three times.*

3. **Inspiration:** *Take a full breath in, slowly drawing revitalizing dragon energy up through your feet and into your body, filling every cell with clarity and the golden light of inspiration. Repeat three times.*

B. **Using the Silver moon and the Golden Sun to Cleanse, Inspire and Revitalize.**

This meditation is wonderful for any of us whose busy lives make us just want to flop onto our beds and find some relief in sleep. But if we can clear our thoughts and energies first, using the powerful colors, silver and gold, we'll find that sleep will be far more refreshing and we'll awake inspired and revitalized in the morning.

1. ***Empty***: *Imagine a huge silvery watery moon above your head. Let it pass down through your body, washing away old emotions, unwelcome energies and unnecessary thoughts. The water of the moon is cooling, calming and refreshing. Pay particular attention to your womb or sacral chakra, releasing emotions you may have felt or picked up from difficult encounters during the day. If you wish, you can actually stand in a shower, seeing the water as silvery moon droplets.*

2. ***Connect***: *When you go to bed, lie on your back for a moment and imagine lying in the loving arms of your soul, with your heart resonating with the rhythm of your soul. Know all is well.*

3. ***Be Inspired***: *As you step out of bed in the morning, send your roots into Mother Earth, feeling her nurturing soil offer support and security to you and your roots. Now, imagine the golden sun beneath your feet and fill yourself with golden creative energy as if the sun is rising through you. When the golden light reaches the top of your head, let it shower out and down over your body, creating a bubble of creative energy around you, which will be your source of inspiration and energy throughout the day.*

C. **Rooting ourselves into Mother Earth** stabilizes our energy allowing us to connect with more ease to our intuitive knowing. (Repeat the process you learned in chapter 8).

Once we know how to quiet our mind and connect to our soul, you'll be surprised at the many intuitive messengers available to you:

These include:

1. *Understanding the **message of illness**: what does your body - your greatest friend - want you to hear?*

2. ***Reading an insightful paragraph*** *in a book that has been on your shelf unread for years.*

3. ***Receiving a flyer*** *through the mail from an organization to which you've never subscribed.*

4. ***Sitting next to a stranger*** *in a meeting who tells you something that begins the next stage of your journey.*

Here are some well-honed tips to enhance the process of listening to and following through on your Intuitive insights. Fill in the gaps below with magical insights you receive when listening to your intuition.

1. **Three-time rule**: If, for instance, you hear about an event three times in a short space of time, act on this intuitive hit and take action by registering for the event.

2. **Instant answer**: If you're looking for a *yes* or *no* answer to a question such as *should I take a vacation or sell my home,* state the question clearly and then say to yourself: *The answer will appear in the next twenty minutes.* Now, with no expectations, take a walk and, using your outer senses, allow yourself to be intuitively drawn toward something you see, read, or hear in the present environment. Listen to the answer and make a note, trying not to say: *I don't like that answer, send me another!*
Question:

Answer

3. **Create a poem** beginning with the words *If my soul could speak to me today, it would say . . .*

Let your soul speak to you, flowing without the need for rhyme or technique. Read it out loud to yourself.

4. **Write a question** with your dominant hand and then the answer it with your non-dominant hand. This moves the intellectual mind out of way, allowing the intuition to speak.
   Question:

   Answer

5. **If you're ready to make changes in your life** but don't know which way to turn, say clearly to the spirit world or Universe before you

go to sleep: *Close all the doors that are not in harmony with my soul and open, or leave open, those that are.*

Just don't blame me if your life changes quickly:

It's just a sign as to how much you are loved by the Great Mother!

CHAPTER 28

The Healing Power of Compassion

When women create a sacred space of trust and respect, where judgments are left outside and we listen with our hearts and wombs not our heads, we generate one of the most powerful healing forces in the universe: *compassion.*

Such healing doesn't involve thinking, fixing, rescuing, or doing something, but sitting with the feelings or emotions of another woman or sister of the heart- true compassion. This is more difficult than you may imagine, as our mind constantly wants to offer suggestions or talk about our experiences. To sit in compassion, we first need to be able to empty our mind, and our ego's need to be heard or be helpful. Only in the no-thingness of mystery can we meet someone in our nakedness, with nothing to hide and nothing to gain.

As Rumi said: *Out beyond ideas of wrongdoing and rightdoing there is a field. I'll meet you there.*

Listening to our "sisters" with our hearts and wombs, we become aware that even though we've not been through exactly the same experience that they have, we've felt the same feelings. Then I can honestly say: *I see you, I hear your heart, I feel your pain, I know who you are, and I love you.* With these honest words and feelings, the healing process begins, not only for this woman but for all women who have ever felt the same pain or experienced the same wound.

This is another facet of the blood mysteries. When the flowing red water dissolves away any barriers that keep us separate from each other, the simple process of sharing of feelings—whether joy, laughter, or pain—brings profound healing not only to the individual but also to the last seven generations and the next seven generations of children still to be born.

This is the power of compassion.
This is the power of women together healing the world

Healing Ritual

Here's a lovely distant healing meditation which you can use whenever you want to bring healing to female friend or relative or sister of the heart through the power of compassion. You can also adapt it to being in the presence of a woman who needs healing, when the second stage can be spoken out loud.

The meditation follows the same three phases of the moon-time ritual:

a. **Empty:** *Imagine standing together in a beautiful, shallow pool of seawater, which is constantly being renewed by the gentle waves of Mother Ocean. Allow your bodies to be bathed by the healing power of the water, which starts to dissolve away pain and difficult emotions, and breaks down any separation between you.*

b. **Connect:** *Now, having stepped out of the pool, imagine that you are both sitting comfortably by the pool, wrapped in soft, warm shawls. Let her tell her story, expressing feelings, not just with words, but through her body and face. Be still, for it is not your role to react or judge but to witness. As your awareness remains in your heart and womb, you may feel the same emotions, mirroring those being expressed.*

Then you can say:

- *I see you (point to your eyes and then hers)*

- *I hear your heart (imagining one of your hands touching your heart and the other hand touching her heart)*

- *I feel your pain (with one hand on your womb and one on hers)*

- *I know who you are (pointing your hands to the dragon Earth grid)*

- *I love you (imagining giving her a hug). I am another one of you.*

c. **Inspiration:** *Show this sister of the heart how to root herself into Mother Earth and then how to draw the cleansing and creative golden dragon energy up into her womb, then into her heart and finally into her crown empowering her with new energy to heal, stand strong, be seen, and be free. To complete the meditation, see the golden light of connectivity flow out to embrace all women who suffer the same pain or wounds, creating a powerful spiral of healing in the name of togetherness and compassion.*

Personal Healing

Standing in front of a mirror say:

- *I see me* (pointing to our eyes)

- *I hear my heart* (crossing our hands across our heart chakra)

- *I feel my feelings* (placing our hands on our womb or sacral chakra)

- *I know and trust me* (pointing toward the Earth and the dragon grid)

- *I love me* (giving ourselves a hug).

Finally, in front of the mirror and using the same hand movements, we can feel the loving embrace of the Spirit world and Great Mother by saying:

I am seen, my heart is heard, my feelings are felt, I am known for who I am and I am loved.

These are very powerful affirmations!

CHAPTER 29

Together We Can Move Mountains

One of the Greatest Strengths of Women is our Power to Connect and to Love; Togetherness.

If you've ever been part of a group of women meeting for the first time, you'll notice that our immediate response is to find points of common interest so we can begin to bond: *I love your shoes, I'm really enjoying this show* or *do you have children?* It might sound superficial to an outsider but we're focused on our purpose; we know that bonding and togetherness bring us strength and healing. Unlike men who tend to feel secure when personal space is respected, women feel safe when feelings and stories are shared. This builds trust and makes us feel we're not alone. However, if we detect the merest whiff that we're being "fixed" or judged—masculine energy—then we'll quickly close our shell, protecting our most susceptible self.

Tending and Befriending

This innate desire to bond and share reflects the inclination for women to gather and talk to one another in stressful situations rather than to activate the fight-or-flight response. UCLA psychologist Dr. Shelley Taylor called this reaction *tending and befriending,* suggesting it arises due to increased levels of the love hormone, oxytocin, released during stress.

Whereas testosterone inhibits oxytocin's influence, its effects are enhanced in the presence of estrogen, leading to greater connection, relaxation, and trust—strength in numbers. Oxytocin levels are further increased and anxiety reduced through the stimulation of our senses, including listening, touching, seeing, and feeling. When we're not heard, touched, seen, or allowed to share our feelings, our anxiety levels escalate. Unfortunately, in today's busy world, there's often too little time for eye to eye contact or heart-centered conversation, leaving many women feeling socially isolated. Texting, e-mailing, and tweeting just don't meet this need.

Forming Trusting Relationships

As we've learned, when a child suckles at the breast there's an outpouring of oxytocin into the bloodstreams of both mother and baby, leading to a strengthening of the bond between the two and increasing the mother's desire to protect and care for her child. Even beyond breastfeeding, oxytocin levels remain at optimal levels through the mother's gentle touch, loving eye contact, and sweet words of comfort. Such mother-child bonding in the first few months of life influences our ability to develop intimate and trustworthy relationships as an adult. Babies who have a poor connection with their mothers often grow up with a fear of rejection, trust issues (especially around women), and being socially isolated.

All is not lost, as it's now known that building strong and caring relationships with women friends or looking into the eyes of a pet will elevate our deficient oxytocin levels. But to fully understand this lack of trust between women and how this is impacting families and corporations even today, we have to step back thousands of years, to the rise of the patriarchy around 1500 BCE.

Inherited Distrust of Other Women

Prior to 1500 BCE, most ancient cultures followed the ideals of matrilineality, wherein inheritance of titles and property are passed down through the female line. Women generally lived in communities, sharing the raising of their children and becoming financially wealthy through their feminine gifts and talents. Although men were also part of the community there were no contracted partnerships between men and women; both free to sleep and live with anyone they chose.

If a woman decided to have a child, she would select a man and, nine months later, would give birth, without expecting the father to be part of the child's life, given that the whole tribe raised the child. Indeed, in ancient times, men probably didn't even know that the one night of pleasure months before had led to the birth, causing women to be held in even higher esteem as miraculous creators of life.

However, no man could make a claim on the child, for paternity was always in doubt. If a woman decided to end a relationship, she would simply leave the man's clothes at the door of her house and he would be expected to leave. As you can imagine, over time this arrangement began to irritate the patriarchy. Thus they enacted new laws that dismantled the communities, forbade sex before marriage, and created today's commonly used marriage contract.

This contract states: one man, one wife, with all titles and property passing down through the paternal line, allowing the father to claim rights to the child's inheritance. As is often the case, even today, the changes were all about money and power and never about what was best for the child.

Today, there are still a few cultures where matrilineality is practiced, but there are also societies that take ownership of women to a whole new level, with men believing they have a right to tell a woman what to do, say, and wear, in the name of her honor.

Women Compete

Over time, with this new marriage contract, women saw their freedom to work and to be financially secure diminish. Whereas in the past, many women could happily share the pleasures of one man, now they were living in a harem-like set up. Women had to compete with each other to be the favorite wife in the hopes of securing a decent future for their children. We can only imagine what devious tricks our female ancestors must have played on each other when the well-being of their child was at stake!

Fast-forward three thousand years and women are still competing for the favors of men, fighting over children or willing to destroy another woman's reputation in order to win. If you don't believe me, just look around. One of the most common scenarios is when a woman wants to sleep with another woman's husband. She's only too happy to hear her lover describe his wife in unsavory terms, for this makes her number 1 wife or concubine, handing men the power to divide and conquer.

I have a suggestion that would change the face of the world overnight: *If you want to sleep with a married man, go and ask his wife first.* You may be surprised by her reply, especially when she says: *Yes, please do, I could do with a rest!* Only in this way will power be back in the hands of women who collectively want to provide the most secure and carefree future for *all* children.

Reflect on your own feelings towards women by answering these questions:

1. *What is precious about my intimate female relationships?*

2. *What do I look for in female relationships?*

3. *What may cause me not to trust women?*

4. *Where have I been hurt by other women?*

5. *What qualities do I possess that I wouldn't want other women to see in me?*

6. *What do I plan to change today that will allow me to get closer to other women?*

CHAPTER 30

The Queen Bee

This handbook of women's mysteries would not be complete without mention of the Queen Bee. My attention was drawn to the link between women and the bee during my first trip to the tiny islands of Malta and Gozo in the Mediterranean Sea. At the entrance to the first temple I visited, I saw stone lintels covered by rows of tiny hexagrams, which reminded me of a beehive with its tiny cells. As I continued my journey around the islands, I was greeted by more and more references to bees, whether in objects, drawings or, as in the underground hypogeum, secluded places where individuals would come to dream.

It was only later that I learned that the islands of Malta and Gozo are thought to be mountaintops that once belonged to the drowned civilization of Atlantis. The female leader of Atlantis was known as the *Queen Bee*, using the fifty-plus stone temples for both the downloading of information into the Earth and as the means to enter other realms of existence; a two-way transporter room from the realms of *Star Trek*.

Throughout history and in various cultures—including the Maya, the aboriginals of Australia, the Egyptians, the Sumerians, the Babylonians, the Minoan, and the ancient Greeks—gods and humans have paid reverence to the *humble honeybee*, as the doorkeeper to other realms. Honey has extraordinary, preservative properties; it never decays. For this reason, many ancient cultures left pots of honey with the corpse, so the deceased could be nourished on their journey through the afterlife by this eternal food of the gods.

For women, it is the Queen Bee who watches over us as we hold our chalice above our head and open ourselves up to the spark of inspiration from the multiple dimensions of our imagination. It is she who connects the soul of the baby to the soul of the mother, and the soul of the man during sex to his oneness or full potential. She guides us during every rite of passage—especially menarche and menopause—as we transition from one stage of life to the next, similar to the egg, larva, and pupa stages of the bee. She prods us with her sting when we procrastinate or hesitate too long. When we hum, we're calling on her to be with us, so we don't get lost in our thoughts or illusions. She reminds us that however far we travel away from the hive, her love will make sure there's always a *beeline home* again.

Reaching the Climax of the Mysteries

Little is known about the actual ceremony which took place annually in the city of Eleusis for almost two thousand years, such was the level of secrecy and respect which surrounded the Mysteries. We do know that the climax of the ceremony took place in the initiation hall where the high priestesses produced a brilliant light which symbolized the eternal light of life beyond death.

As women, we have the chance to experience this every month whether during our period or during the three dark moon days. Then we can release our hold on the outer world and, held by our rootedness into Mother Earth, climb our own serpentine ladder and pass through the doorway guarded by the Queen Bee to meet ourselves as our multi-dimensional or mysterious selves. Here we meet our soul family and those from the spirit world who love and support us and remember that, in reality, there is no separation; everything is connected and everything is love.

Women are the keepers of mystery; we are the ones who have the courage to step into the unknown every month to keep alight the creative fires. It's also good to remember that life is like floating on an ocean. Sometimes the waves will take us deep down when the way ahead appears dark, but if we just wait, we'll be carried up on top of the next wave and, with a whoop of joy, suddenly everything makes sense. Mother Earth has and will survive anything humans throw at her. She is evolving at this time, and by keeping our roots firmly planted in her and allowing love to keep us connected to our soul and our mysterious self, we will meet the challenges life throws at us and will successfully surf the waves of change.

Now on completing this Handbook, what were the ten most important messages you embraced into your heart, and plan to embody from this moment onwards:

1.

2.

3.

4.

5.

6.

7.

8.

9.

10.

FROM THE AUTHOR

Christine Page MD

I hope you have enjoyed embracing these Women's Mysteries and learning more about yourself.

Five valuable meditations are available to you as MP3 downloads or on a CD, created to help you deepen your embodiment of the Mysteries. These can be purchased by going to the store on www.christinepage.com

You may also be interested in diving deeper into these Ancient Mysteries, by joining me on my online course, *Women's Mysteries for the Modern Woman.*

https://www.christinepage.com/womens-mysteries/

Also available on my store in hardcopy, audio and digital formats:
- *Healing Power of the Sacred Woman*
- *Frontiers of Health*
- *Beyond the Obvious*
- *Mirror of Existence*
- *Mind. Body, Spirit Workbook*
- *Spiritual Alchemy*
- *The Return of the Great Mother*